STUDY GUl

for use with

MARKETING
FOUNDATIONS
AND
APPLICATIONS

Carolyn Siegel
Eastern Kentucky University

IRWIN
MIRROR PRESS

Chicago • Bogotá • Boston • Buenos Aires • Caracas
London • Madrid • Mexico City • Sydney • Toronto

©Richard D. Irwin, a Times Mirror Higher Education Group, Inc. company, 1996

Printed in the United States of America.

ISBN 0-256-20834-4

1 2 3 4 5 6 7 8 9 0 P 2 1 0 9 8 7 6 5

PREFACE

Marketing is such a complex, multifaceted subject that some aspect of it is bound to engage your interest. Marketing is exciting to study because what you learn in the classroom can be applied almost immediately to experiences in your daily life. Marketing is everywhere and inescapable. It is personal, yet also extremely important to business and society. Marketing is changing to meet the challenges of the Information Revolution. It will be a significant factor that helps decide how well businesses and organizations perform in the next century.

This *Study Guide* was written to facilitate your study of marketing and to accompany Marketing: Foundations and Applications. The Guide begins appropriately with **Part I: Starting Points**. The materials in this section are designed to accomplish several purposes.

Part I: 1. **To help you become a better student.** This section discusses the nuts and bolts of what it takes to become a better student, from taking notes to taking exams. It describes strategies for getting the most from your class, textbook, and *Study Guide*. Several exercises in the section give you an opportunity to assess your strengths and weaknesses as a student, then formulate goals for enhancing the strengths and correcting the weaknesses.

2. **To introduce you to the Internet.** The Internet has the capacity to revolutionize the way people communicate, retrieve information, and market products. In this section you will learn about the history and evolution of the Internet, Internet communication, etiquette on the Internet (Netiquette), and some places to visit once you get started.

3. **To launch your career exploration.** This section challenges you to look beyond the classroom and open your eyes to career opportunities in marketing. You will be asked to perform an analysis of your employment strengths and weaknesses, and assess the opportunities and threats in the present job environment. You will recognize this device as the SWOT analysis, commonly used by businesses and adapted here for your benefit. Instructions are provided for designing your own marketing plan to market yourself to a prospective employer, along with tips on writing a resume and interviewing.

Part II: Mastering Marketing contains individual study guides for the fifteen chapters in the textbook. Each chapter is organized to accompany and match the textbook. Abundant opportunities are provided for you to ask and answer questions that are keyed to chapter contents. Conscientiously working through the study guides and accompanying textbook chapters will enhance understanding, learning, and recall.

Part III: Answers To Study Guide "Test Yourself" Questions provides answer keys to questions posed at the end of each chapter study guide. These questions supplement the questions in your textbook.

Some Observations On Becoming A Better Student

You can become better at the job of being a student, whether you are a full-time or part-time, traditional or non-traditional student. You can learn from experience, from teachers, by observing other students, and through reading, including the materials in this section of the *Study Guide*. From years of experience as a student and teacher, as well as observations of my own students, I would like to pass along some tips that may help you become a better student.

Know What To Expect: From the beginning of the term, understand what your instructor expects from you and be realistic about the time and effort that will be needed to meet those expectations. Understand what is expected from you in this *Guide* and make a commitment to yourself that you will meet those expectations. Understand what will be expected from you in the future as an employee. View this class as an opportunity to begin acquiring the knowledge, skills, and ability that will help make you a more desirable employee.

Take Responsibility: You are responsible for your own success. You can achieve your learning goals through commitment and smart work. Change and grow through this learning opportunity and make a commitment to yourself that you will end the term a better student than when you began it.

Show Enthusiasm: Negativism is a self-fulfilling prophecy. Go into your class with a positive, "can do" attitude. Pledge to yourself that you will succeed, then work hard and smart to make sure it happens. Make it your mantra and goal: "I will succeed."

Be Organized: Being organized is tough for many people, but you must be organized to succeed at work and school. Use your time in this class to develop your organizational skills. Consider it an investment, both in becoming a better student and for your future, as a better employee.

Get The Most From Your Marketing Class: Many things that you will learn in marketing class can be applied in your daily life. View this class as an opportunity to find meaningful applications that can help you become a more knowledgeable consumer and a more effective businessperson. You may discover that it sets you on the path toward a rewarding career as a marketing professional.

All suggestions in this *Study Guide* may not be equally helpful to you. Try them, see what works, and adopt the best as your own. I hope you enjoy learning about marketing and do well in class. If you find that marketing is the career for you, I wish you a long, satisfying, meaningful life as a marketer.

CONTENTS

PART I
STARTING POINTS

■ **Becoming A Better Student**

Assessing Yourself

Setting Goals

Managing Time

Getting The Most From Your Textbook

Listening

Studying

Taking Notes

Taking Tests

Asking Questions

Staying Healthy

■ **The Internet**

History And Evolution

Internet Communication

Netiquette

Getting Started

■ **Launching Your Career: Marketing Yourself To Prospective Employers**

Exploring Marketing Careers

Assessing Your Employability

Identifying How You'll Benefit An Employer

Your Own Marketing Plan

Writing A Resume

Developing Interviewing Skills

Career Resources

References

BECOMING A BETTER STUDENT

What are you going to get out of this marketing class? Are you here to find out if a career in marketing is right for you? Do you want to learn how to market your business or yourself? Are you in a marketing class because it is required in your program of study?

Whatever your reasons for being here, you can get more out of this class, as well as other classes, by studying and applying what you learn in this section. You *CAN* become a better student and by doing so, help position yourself for a more promising future. Research has shown convincingly that generally, educated people earn more and get better jobs. The rewards are clearly within reach of people who are motivated to make a sustained, well-directed effort.

■ **Becoming A Better Student is organized into the following sections.**

- Assessing yourself
- Setting goals
- Managing time
- Getting the most from your textbook
- Studying
- Listening
- Taking notes
- Taking tests
- Asking questions
- Staying healthy

BECOMING A BETTER STUDENT: ASSESSING YOURSELF

Before you can become better at something, you have to know where you are at the start. That is where we are now — at a point of self-discovery. This section provides you with an opportunity to honestly assess yourself as a student, your strengths and weaknesses, the opportunities and rewards that being a better student may bring, and the threats to your becoming a better student. This is a personal and private evaluation, for your eyes only. After you complete the analysis, invest in yourself by working hard to eliminate or reduce weaknesses and enhance your strengths.

In the S-W Grid on the next page, list what you honestly feel are your strengths (S) and weaknesses (W) as a student. For example, consider your level of *motivation*, sense of *responsibility*, and *skills* in such areas as

- organizing
- reading
- listening
- writing
- note taking
- studying
- working with others
- managing time
- test taking

Some of these areas may represent your strengths; others may be weaknesses. You may feel that you are good at studying, but can't seem to find the time to do it. So, studying skills are a strength, while time management is a weakness. You may be great at studying, but delay studying until the night before a test.

Procrastination is definitely a weakness in this case, for you may pass the test but won't retain the information.

Once you have listed your strengths and weaknesses, rank order them. In the "Strengths" cell, if you believe your top strength is an ability to concentrate, mark it "1". In the "Weakness" cell, if your worst weakness is your disorganization, mark it "1". When you have finished ranking all the items in the S-W Grid, you will have identified a set of personal characteristics whose strengths you intend to enhance and whose weaknesses you intend to improve.

S-W GRID

My Strengths As A Student	My Weaknesses As A Student

It is also useful to expand your self-assessment to include an analysis of the threats to your becoming a better student and the opportunities or rewards that may come your way if you do. To help you focus your thoughts, an O-T Grid on the next page provides space for you to list Opportunities and Threats. Some opportunities/rewards that you might consider relate to how becoming a better student will affect your grades, your academic standing, your self-esteem, family and friends' opinions of you, your ability to find a good internship, choice of major, and your options for jobs and a career. Threats to your becoming a better student may include the effects of having to attend school part-time and work full-time, demands placed on you by family and friends, or the effects of a long commute to school. Rank order the O-T items the same way you did the items in the S-W Grid, beginning with number "1".

O-T GRID

Opportunities	Threats

Through this self-assessment, you should have achieved a more honest view of where you are and how far you have to go to become a better student. In the next section, we talk about setting goals for success.

BECOMING A BETTER STUDENT: SETTING GOALS

A goal is something we try to achieve at the end of one or more actions. If I set a personal weight loss goal, I start from knowledge of my present weight (*at XXX pounds, too much!*), set a target weight (*20 pounds less*), and begin taking positive steps (*eat less, exercise more*) to achieve my weight goal. At points in between, I weigh myself, which provides feedback, note my progress and give myself small rewards for success.

Most of us have many different personal and professional goals operating at the same time. Sometimes these goals complement one another, other times they may conflict. It is well known that in school and work settings, goals are important factors in motivating people to achieve improved performance. By setting goals we focus our attention and direct our energies toward the actions that will allow us to reach the goals we've set. Unfortunately, too often we set "New Year's Resolution" goals that disappear about as fast as memories of having set them.

What do we know about goals?

- People set multiple goals that operate concurrently
- The time required to achieve goals varies, from very short term to intermediate and long term
- Not all goals are of equal importance, some have priority over others
- Personal goals are unique to the person
- Personal and professional goals may be incongruent and contradictory, and can conflict
- Personal goals can conflict
- In the workplace, goals that are consensually agreed to usually result in higher achievement than goals that are imposed on a group by others
- Hard, yet realistic, achievable goals result in better performance than easy goals
- Quantitative goals are easier to monitor than qualitative goals, for example it is clear that if I lose 20 pounds, my goal has been achieved, whereas a goal of "losing some weight" is more difficult to measure
- Specific written goals result in better performance than vague, unwritten goals
- Goals often must be revised
- New goals are continuously being set
- Feedback is important because it provides information on how successful you are in working toward achieving a goal
- When faced with a difficult goal, it is sometimes best to break it into smaller subgoals that can be achieved sequentially

Now, let's apply this goal setting information to your S-W and O-T Grids. We'll assume that you are already committed to enhancing your strengths, so concentrate on your weaknesses from the S-W Grid. Likewise, concentrate on the threats from the O-T Grid, because they can undermine your opportunities and rewards.

Realistically, there are some weaknesses and threats that may be beyond your control at this time. However, it is just as likely that there are others that lend themselves to goal setting actions. Although no guarantee of success can ever be made in such activities, often students find that by directing their attention to what *should* be done to achieve their goals, they are taking the first step toward doing so.

You can work through the goal setting process by completing the Goal Setting form. Begin with your number "1" weakness, then continue with the other weaknesses and threats until you have a clear understanding of the goal setting process and how it relates to your becoming a better student.

GOAL SETTING FORM

1. Goal

Identify one goal for yourself for the coming academic term. If it relates to a weakness, restate it in a positive way. For example, *"My goal is to use my study time more effectively, setting aside two hours to study for every hour I spend in class."* Make the goal clear, hard but achievable, and if at all possible, measurable. Write it out since this strengthens your commitment.

My goal is to _____

_____.

2. Timing

Identify the time frame required to achieve this goal. Goals may take several weeks, months, or even a year or more to accomplish. For example, *"I will begin the first week of class and study two hours Tuesday and Thursday evenings and two hours on Sunday. I will mark my study times on a calendar and check off every day I study so I can track my weekly progress over the term."*

Time frame is _____

_____.

3. Difficulty

How difficult will it be for you to achieve this goal? For example, *"This is a difficult goal to achieve because I will have to make my family understand that for these hours I must study and cannot be disturbed. I will have to forgo other activities in order to carve out the time to study. This includes rearranging my work schedule to leave Tuesday and Thursday evenings for studying."*

Difficulty is_____

_____.

4. Benefits

What benefits will you receive from achieving this goal? For example, *"If I study using this schedule, I will be able to review class notes and bring questions to class to clarify what I do not understand. If I read chapters in advance, I will gain more from class discussion because I'll understand more of what the instructor is saying. If I study steadily throughout the term, I won't panic because I have to cram the night before a test."*

Benefits are_____

_____.

5. Actions

What actions will you have to take in order to achieve this goal?

For example, *"I will have to make my family understand about my study times. I will have to shut the door to my study area. I will have to ignore telephone calls and other distractions. I will have to be prepared to study so I don't waste time. I will have to rearrange my work schedule."*

Actions are _____

_____.

6. Feedback

What measures will provide feedback, letting you know how well you are working toward achieving the goal? For example, *"I will maintain a calendar where I check off each study time that I complete. I will make notes to myself on the calendar each time that I recognize a benefit that can be traced to my study schedule."*

Measures are _____

_____.

7. Resources

What resources will you need to achieve this goal? For example, *"I will need to establish a study area in my home where I can work undisturbed. I will have to organize my study area so that I have ready access to my textbook, this Study Guide, paper, pencils, and other materials. I will need access to a library, either a traditional library or one that is on-line."*

Resources needed _____

_____.

8. Priority

What is the priority of this goal compared to others? For example, *"This is my top priority. My biggest weakness has been that I don't study enough, regularly, or effectively. I usually read a little here and there, then cram the night before a test. As a result, I don't get as much from class as I should. If I improve my study skills, it will help me become a better student. It will also help me become more marketable to an employer because I will have demonstrated self-discipline and taken responsibility for my success."*

Priority is _____

_____.

Use the matrix on the next page to organize your goals for the term. Set priorities for achieving these goals and recognize that you may have to sacrifice low priority goals, at least temporarily, in order to concentrate on achieving top priority goals. Realize that some goals are more elusive than others and may be harder to achieve. If you need more space for additional goals, copy the matrix.

MY TERM GOALS

	Goal 1	Goal 2	Goal 3	Goal 4
1. Goal				
2. Timing				
3. Difficulty				
4. Benefits				
5. Actions				
6. Feedback (Measures)				
7. Resources				
8. Priority				

BECOMING A BETTER STUDENT: MANAGING TIME

Time is...

Short	There's never enough of it.
Long	Some things seem to take forever.
Fast	It goes by far too fast when you're having fun.
Slow	It drags when you want it to pass.
Rich	We spend it recklessly, as if we have unlimited quantities.
Poor	We complain about being starved for time.
Divisible	It can be broken into smaller bits.
Extended	It is infinite, as in the ages.
Nonrenewable	Once used, it is gone forever.
Regretted	When it goes by unnoticed.
Enlivening	When it brings delights.
Unpredictable	You can't predict when you'll have too much or too little.
Variable	Older people complain that time passes too quickly; younger ones complain it doesn't pass quickly enough.
Unbiased	Regardless of race, color, creed, religion, or nationality, we all have 24 hours in a day and 60 minutes in an hour.

How will you find the *time* to achieve the goals you've set for yourself on the way to becoming a better student? Since most people are time-starved, this is a serious question. You can start by setting priorities, ration the time you do have to ensure that your most important goals are acted on. Try some of the following **Time Tips** and adopt what works for you.

- Set your activities by your inner clock. If you think best in the morning, then set aside morning time for intellectual activities such as studying. If you have a "low" time in the late afternoon, set that time aside for activities that don't require creativity, concentration, or mental work, like watching television or relaxing with a pick-up game of basketball. Observe your own biological pattern of high and low energy times by making a time chart of a waking day. From the time you rise until you retire, do a time check every hour and track your bio-clock peaks and valleys. Then match your bio-clock against your daily activities, those over which you have no control and others which you can control. Identify time periods where you should study, because it is a mental peak time, and make sure that you do so. Avoid low energy times for mental activities as you may spend the time but learn little.

- Organize your time. Make lists of things that must be done and others that can wait. A "To Do" list is an essential part of organizing your activities. Cluster activities in order to get more accomplished in a time period. For example, if you have to run to the post office to pick up stamps, as long as you'll be out anyway, add several other nearby errands so you can compress your errands and reduce travel time. Plan ahead, establish a study pattern. For example, "If this is Tuesday, it is study night." This patterning process will help you become accustomed to studying at specific times.

- Use your time wisely: Don't waste it. Identify your main time wasters and reduce or eliminate them. For example, television and video games can be entertaining, but they also can waste time. Ration your entertainment time and use it to reward yourself when you deserve it for accomplishing a goal. Avoid long telephone calls and even answering the telephone when you are in the middle of studying. Buy an answering machine so you can return calls later instead of interrupting your concentration. Having a social life is important, but so is making progress toward achieving your professional goals. Learn to use your time wisely and you should have enough time for most of what you need to do.

- Deal with procrastination. A procrastinator is good at delays, postponing tasks until it is often too late to do them. If you are a procrastinator, learn to deal with it. Break tasks into smaller units in order to reduce the magnitude of what must be accomplished. Give yourself small rewards for accomplishing tasks. Create a good work environment for yourself so you won't dread getting to work. Analyze why you are procrastinating, then try to reduce or eliminate the core problem.

BECOMING A BETTER STUDENT: GETTING THE MOST FROM YOUR TEXTBOOK

A considerable amount of effort and time went into the development of your textbook and this *Study Guide*. You owe it to yourself to get the most you can from both. Here are some tips for ensuring that you do.

- Know the due dates for each chapter. As soon as you get a class syllabus, note the dates by which each chapter must be read. Keep a term calendar in your study area and mark the chapter due dates on the calendar, in your textbook, and this *Study Guide*.

- Scan before you read. It helps to identify the subject of a chapter before you begin to read and study it in depth. In order to "get the lay of the land", quickly scan the chapter before you read it. Look at the chapter objectives in the front of the chapter, then browse the chapter without underlining, highlighting, or taking notes. Look at the figures and pictures. Scan each of the boxed areas. By the time you get to the last page, you should have a very good mental view of the chapter's contents. Do the same with the *Study Guide* so you will know what information will be required to answer the questions in each section.

- Read for content and details. After scanning, read the chapter for details, carefully studying each section and highlighting key terms and points. Write notes in the margins, underline important passages, and summarize the contents of each box in a few words written beside it.

- Use the numbered chapter objectives as study guides. Each of the fifteen chapters is organized around numbered key learning objectives. These numbered objectives are stated at the beginning of the chapter and form the major subsections within the chapter. The chapter summary statements at the end of the chapter correspond to the numbered objectives. The chapter sections in this *Study Guide* also are keyed to the chapter numbered objectives. Let these objectives serve as your study guides. Restate them in question form and, after you have read the section, test your mastery of it by answering the question.

- Study all chapter boxes, figures, and activities. Even if these materials are not singled out in class, make them part of your studies. Read each chapter box, including **Consumer Insight, Marketing on the Internet**, and **International Marketing** because they will add to your understanding of marketing and give you a broader base of knowledge that you can call on to answer test questions. Even if your instructor does not assign a **Marketing Application** as a class project, read it and think about how you would carry out the application if it had been assigned.

- Answer the questions. This *Study Guide* provides space for you to answer the **Check Your Understanding** and **Discussion Questions**, define **Key Terms**, respond to **What Do You Think?**, and answer the **Mini-Case** questions. Asking and answering questions are an important part of understanding, learning, and recall. Some of the questions are repeated to aid recall and because your answers should gain complexity as you learn more. For example, a question from an early **Check Your Understanding** may reappear as a **Discussion Question** at the end of the chapter. The second answer should reflect the additional knowledge you've gained after reading the entire chapter and the repetition should help embed the information in your memory and aid later recall.

- Talk back to the book! As you read, underline, highlight, circle, and write comments in the margins as you find information that is key to your understanding of the chapter. Use highlighters in different colors to mark key terms, important phrases, and numbered objectives.

- Use the *Study Guide* as you read the textbook. Because the *Study Guide* is organized to accompany the textbook, using it will save you time and effort in organizing your studying, concentrating your thoughts, understanding, and learning. It is an extension of your textbook and specifically designed to make learning easier. Place the *Study Guide* chapter beside you as you read the corresponding textbook chapter so it is readily available for answering questions as they appear in the text. If you separate the chapters in the *Study Guide*, make a file folder for each chapter and place the *Study Guide* pages in the folder where they can be kept until needed later. Alternately, place them in a three ring notebook binder with separate dividers for each chapter.

BECOMING A BETTER STUDENT: LISTENING

Most students never have a class in listening; they are just expected to do it. Unfortunately, while we do a lot of it, often it's not done well. Listening is the key to understanding, yet we listen at only about a 25 percent level of efficiency. Part of the problem is that people can speak at an average rate of 100 to 250 words per minute, while we listen at an average rate up to 500 words per minute. This discrepancy helps explain why our minds sometimes wander and we don't listen effectively.

Listening in class is an essential part of becoming a better student. Begin by being ready to listen. This means getting to class and settling in before it starts. Sit where you can see and hear the instructor. Avoid distractions like the seat by the door where all the hall noises are the loudest. Get enough sleep so you aren't fighting drowsiness while trying to listen. Other **Listening Tips** include:

- Be quiet. Concentrate on what is being said in class. Stop the chatter in your mind. Don't allow yourself to get lost in a daydream or distractions, such as the student next to you who wants to whisper comments about the instructor.

- Maintain eye contact with the speaker, concentrate on what she is saying, and let her know you are interested. This concentration also helps keep your mind from wandering.

- Lean slightly forward in your chair and don't get too comfortable, because this can lead to lost concentration.

- Ignore how the speaker is delivering the message, focus on the message, identify the central ideas and write them down.

- Keep your emotions under control, don't let your feelings undermine your concentration.

- Don't debate the speaker in your mind, save your counterarguments for class discussions.

- Take notes and paraphrase what is said, if you try to write everything you won't be able to listen effectively.

- Pay attention to other cues that underscore the importance of what is said. For example, if the instructor repeats a thought, this gives it emphasis and you should listen for and note the repetition.

- Avoid watching the clock because you will spend more time concentrating on time passing than listening.

- Don't sit with friends because they can be very distracting, particularly if they are not serious students.

- Along with listening, observe nonverbal communication elements. As much as 90 percent of the total impact of a message is associated with nonverbal elements. Verbal and nonverbal communication occur simultaneously in the classroom. They usually are complementary, but sometimes can be contradictory. Be aware of:

  - Vocalization: Vocal elements associated with speaking but not part of spoken language. This includes the tone of voice, its inflection, volume, pauses, and pitch. Often vocalization can provide cues as to the importance of a message.

  - Kinesics: Body language conveys messages through motions, facial expressions, and gestures. Eye contact is particularly important because it indicates that you are receptive to communication.

- Proxemics: Messages are also communicated through spatial relationships. For example, how close or far a student sits from the instructor indicates interest and involvement.

BECOMING A BETTER STUDENT: STUDYING

Good study skills don't just happen, you have to work at building them. It starts with a good physical environment. Identify a place where you can study, preferably where you will be undisturbed and can leave your materials from one study session to the next. Select a chair that gives you good support and a desk or table top at the appropriate height so you can sit comfortably without slouching. You'll need a good light source to illuminate your textbook and this *Study Guide*.

Your study area ideally should have the sound level you find most conducive to concentration. For some people, this means silence. Others require background music as "white noise" to drown out distractions, such as the sound of a television, a telephone conversation, or footsteps.

Supplies should be conveniently at hand. This includes file folders, a three ring notebook, colored highlighters, writing materials, and this *Study Guide*. A clock is very helpful to ensure that you break your studies at regular intervals but also study for the time planned.

Each person must determine their own best study routine. However, the following study tips may help you use your study time more effectively. Studying wiser is much better than just studying more.

- Find a good study area where you can concentrate and be undisturbed.
- Don't lay down while you're studying. For most people, this is simply an invitation to doze off and take a nap.
- Take short study breaks at regular intervals. Don't try to study for hours straight without a break. This dulls the mind and fatigues the body.
- Study with others, members of your class who also take studying seriously. Avoid classmates who consider study time play time.
- Don't wait until the night before an examination to cram. Keep up with your reading and the *Study Guide* questions.
- During any study session, study the hardest or least interesting material first when you are fresh mentally and physically.
- If you find extra time, between classes or while commuting to school (assuming you are not driving), review your class notes.
- Study all materials handed out in class.
- Make files to store chapter materials or use a three ring notebook with dividers to keep materials organized.
- Make a concept map of your readings. You can enhance your studying by making visual connections between key thoughts. For example, Chapter 12 in your textbook introduces the topic of promotion, one of the marketing mix variables. After you have scanned the chapter, chunk the contents into a concept map that organizes and links the concepts. An example is provided on the next page. You can add to the map while you read the chapter in depth. The map provides a quick visual review of the chapter, aides learning and recall. File each chapter concept map in the chapter folder or in its section in the three ring binder. Map neatness doesn't count; thoughtfulness in identifying key concepts and linking them does count.

A Concept Map Of Chapter 12: Understanding Promotion

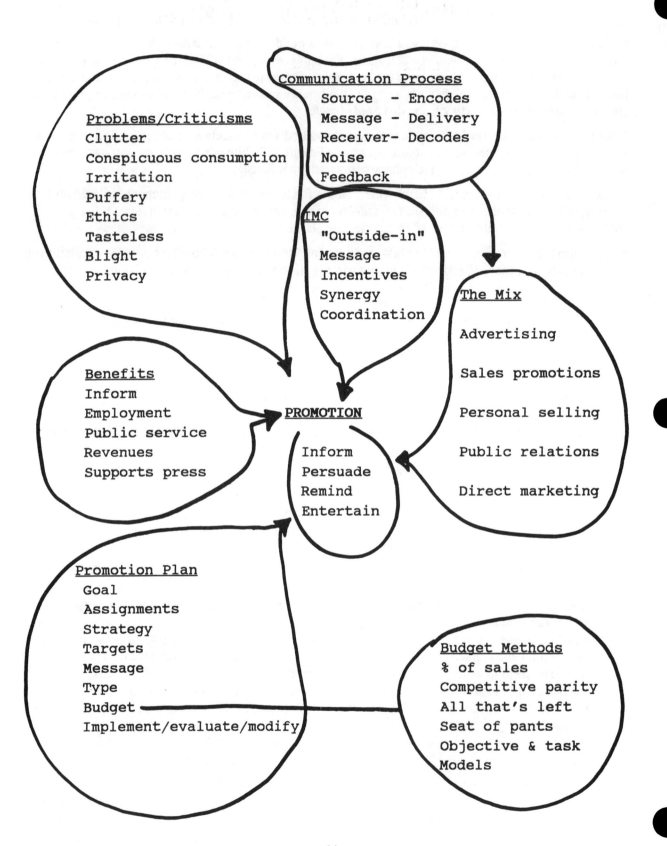

Communication Process
Source - Encodes
Message - Delivery
Receiver- Decodes
Noise
Feedback

Problems/Criticisms
Clutter
Conspicuous consumption
Irritation
Puffery
Ethics
Tasteless
Blight
Privacy

IMC
"Outside-in"
Message
Incentives
Synergy
Coordination

The Mix

Advertising

Sales promotions

Personal selling

Public relations

Direct marketing

Benefits
Inform
Employment
Public service
Revenues
Supports press

PROMOTION

Inform
Persuade
Remind
Entertain

Promotion Plan
Goal
Assignments
Strategy
Targets
Message
Type
Budget
Implement/evaluate/modify

Budget Methods
% of sales
Competitive parity
All that's left
Seat of pants
Objective & task
Models

BECOMING A BETTER STUDENT: TAKING NOTES

Note taking is another area where students are expected to know how to do it without prior training. However, research has shown that note taking completeness may be less than 55 percent, with "A" students recording only 62 percent of the critical information presented in class. Some tips may help you become a better note taker.

- Be organized and prepared to take notes. Have yourself and your materials ready to take notes before class begins. Read the chapter in advance so when it is discussed in class, you are already familiar with the concepts and key terms and don't have to struggle to understand what the instructor is saying.
- Use standard lined or unlined paper. Leave about one and a half inches blank along the right margin of each page. Either fold the page or mark it with a bold line (see example). Write your notes to the left of the line. When you review your notes, make comments in the right margin. Note where key terms are defined or the instructor emphasizes a particular point. Date and number each page so you can easily reassemble your notes if the pages become separated.
- Write quickly, but legibly. If you can't read your own writing, your note taking effort is wasted.@

E = Don't write everything down verbatim. Take short notes, summarize, identify key concepts and terms; paraphrase thoughts. You cannot write as rapidly as someone can speak, so writing notes verbatim can interfere with your listening and learning.

- If your instructor distributes a handout in class, date it and place it with your notes. Be sure to read it carefully, as it may contain information that will be on a test.

```
 _____
|                                   |
|                       12/1/95    |
|                        pg. 1     |
|_____|       
|                          ||       |   <- Write comments in right
|  Take notes here.        ||       |        margin.
|                          ||       |
|                          ||       |
|                          ||       |
|                          ||       |
|                          ||       |
|                          ||       |
|                          ||       |
|                          ||       |
|                          ||       |
|                          ||       |
|                          ||       |
|                          ||       |
|                          ||       |
|                          ||       |
|_____||_____|
```

- Write on only one side of the page so you can go back and add information on the back.
- Don't copy your notes over to make them neater. This is a waste of time and not a good learning device. You are not going to be graded on neatness and copying is not a good substitute for studying.

- Use a three-ring binder for your notes and organize it with dividers separating the chapters. You can also place the corresponding chapters from this *Study Guide* in the binder. Alternately, use separate manila file folders for each chapter.

- Review your notes immediately after class and fill in any blanks. If you cannot remember an item, flag it with a question mark in the right margin and ask the instructor for clarification at the next class meeting.

- Review notes during your study sessions and mark where the instructor emphasizes materials from the textbook.

- If you are in a mass lecture section and the instructor distributes a note-taking guide, use it. It will help reduce writing time and increase listening time. Make your own comments directly on the handout and use additional pages, as needed.

- Use abbreviations to reduce writing time. Some common abbreviations are w/ = with; w/out = without; $\triangle$ = change; bec. = because; & = and; $\therefore$ = therefore.

- Remember, taking notes facilitates learning and reviewing notes facilitates recall. Make the effort to take good notes and then review them.

BECOMING A BETTER STUDENT: TAKING TESTS

The best advice for taking a test is be prepared! If you have studied effectively and sufficiently, taking a test is much easier than if you are ill prepared and panicked. Nothing substitutes for the confidence of knowing that you can handle any question the instructor asks.

Test taking suggestions include:

- As soon as you receive your class syllabus, mark all test dates on your calendar, your textbook, and this *Study Guide*. If the instructor changes a date, make note of the change in each location.

- Study regularly between exams and don't cram at the last minute.

- Review your class notes immediately after you take them, during regular study sessions, and as part of your studying for a test.

- If your instructor offers to provide copies of previous tests, take the opportunity to evaluate the question styles used, particularly the mixture of objective and discussion questions.

- Rescan the textbook chapters that the test will cover, carefully reread any parts that you are uncertain about, look at the notes and underlines you made previously.

- Study your concept maps, add additional information from the textbook or class notes.

- Study with a group of other serious students. Avoid study groups seeking entertainment.

- Be able to answer all questions in the textbook and *Study Guide*.

- The night before the test, get enough sleep so you will be alert during the test. Avoid too much caffeine on the day of the test as it may be overly stimulating and make you edgy.

- Control test stress. Some strategies are offered later in this section.

- Bring a watch to the test and keep an eye on the time. Pace yourself to make sure that you allow enough time for each test section.

- Be on time to the test and settle in before the test is distributed.

- As soon as the instructor gives permission to begin the test, scan it and make sure that you have all the pages and they are readable. Judge how much time will be needed to complete each section,

- Carefully read all instructions and follow them. If the instructions say "Print a T for True and an F for False," do it! If you are answering on a computer scored sheet, fill in the complete circle to ensure that the answer scans accurately.

- Complete easy questions first.

- Mark the hard questions that will need a return visit to complete.
- Read the true and false questions very carefully before you answer. Don't look for patterns in the answers, for example if there are four false answers in a row, that doesn't mean the next answer is true. Look for absolute words such as all, never, and always. Absolute words often hint at a false answer.
- With multiple choice answers, if the instructions tell you to look for the best answer, find it through a process of elimination. Read each answer carefully. If you can mark on the test itself, draw a line through the answers that you can eliminate. This may help you make a final decision about the best answer.
- Read discussion questions carefully, then outline the key points that must be made in the answer. Work from your outline in writing the answer. If you run out of time, an instructor may give you credit if your outline demonstrates that you knew the answer but didn't have time to write it.
- If you have time at the end of the test, reread all your answers and be sure that each one is completed unless the instructor tells you that "guesses" count against you.
- Avoid changing answers unless you are absolutely sure the change is correct.
- When the instructor returns the graded tests, reread all questions, check to ensure no mathematical mistake was made, and ask for a clarification if you don't understand an answer.
- If you receive a bad grade, reexamine how you studied and make a commitment to yourself that next time you will do much better because you will study more effectively.

BECOMING A BETTER STUDENT: ASKING QUESTIONS

Questions are an important part of learning. Asking and answering questions promotes understanding, learning, and recall. Some question tips include:

- Be clear in your own mind why you are asking the question. Typical question goals are to seek or provide information, obtain advice, determine attitudes, allow time to think, and to capture attention.
- Ask one question at a time, avoid overly complex double-barreled questions.
- Don't ask questions to show off.
- Repeat the question in another way if there is a problem in comprehension.
- How you ask is almost as important as what you ask, so be courteous in asking questions in class. If the instructor's answer isn't helpful, wait until after class to seek a clarification.

BECOMING A BETTER STUDENT: STAYING HEALTHY

This may appear to be an odd addition to a section on **Becoming a Better Student,** yet students are notorious for not getting enough sleep, eating junk food, drinking too many caffeine drinks, and all night study binges. Students often experience stress, but may not recognize it or know how to reduce it. Stress is:

An action or situation that places special physical or psychological demands on a person. It is a state of disequilibrium which often is unavoidable. A moderate amount of stress can be a useful motivator.

Stress affects people emotionally, behaviorally, psychologically, and physiologically. Excessive stress can lead to illness, even death. It can contribute to ulcers, migraine headaches, rheumatoid arthritis, backache, and a lowered immune system. Some people thrive on high stress; others avoid it. Being a student is stressful and you should learn how to protect yourself against its harmful effects. Look for such symptoms as:

- Feeling irritable
- Persistent dry mouth, throat, nose, eyes
- Pounding heart

- Compulsive behavior
- Swings in emotion
- Difficulty in concentrating
- Difficulty in falling or staying asleep
- Forgetfulness
- Fatigue
- Procrastination
- Disorganization

Even if you aren't experiencing an extreme response to stress, you should still work to manage the stress you're under.

- Take breaks.
- Read for relaxation.
- Get adequate rest.
- Watch what you eat and try to reduce sugars, fats, and caffeine products while increasing your intake of fruits, vegetables, carbohydrates, and low fat foods.
- Increase your exercise by walking, swimming, jogging, or through aerobics.
- Change your environment, go shopping, to a movie, an art gallery, or other enjoyable destination.
- Listen to and/or play music, sing.
- Play with a pet. Stroking and playing with animals is extremely relaxing for many people.
- Express yourself, talk to yourself and talk out your fears and concerns. Give yourself encouragement and praise.
- Do something for others.

THE INTERNET

HISTORY AND EVOLUTION

References to the Internet are showing up with increased frequency in newspapers, popular magazines, and academic journals. While it is often called the information superhighway, "something" that delivers pizzas and movies on demand, it is important to understand the Internet's history, what it is, and what may be its future. What began initially as a government-directed response to perceived threats to national security is evolving into a commercialized, privatized environment that will affect how marketing is conducted in the next century.

■ **A *Very* Brief History**

The Internet began in the mid-1960s during the Cold War as military researchers sought ways to construct hardened communication systems for maintaining military command-and-control during a nuclear attack. Their work resulted in the development of a packet-switching technology that decomposes messages into components and transmits these bits of data across different routes toward a destination, where they are reassembled into a coherent message.

From its beginnings in the Defense Department's ARPAnet computer network (Advanced Research Projects Agency Network) in 1969, the Internet's reach and focus has steadily expanded as university interest in computers grew throughout the late 1960s and 1970s, and private commercial interest developed in the 1980s and 1990s.

By the mid-1980s, the National Science Foundation had established a network (NSFNet) of supercomputer centers at universities across the country to facilitate collaborative research. These centers allow Local Area Networks (LANs) to internetwork and share computer time using the ARPAnet packet switching technology (Internet Protocol), but not the ARPAnet itself, which was decommissioned in 1990. By 1988, thirteen supercomputers at the center of the networked world formed the backbone of the primarily government-funded Internet. Many regional network routers on the edges provide Internet access to educational institutions. NSF turned over its Internet gateway role to commercial access providers in April 1995.

■ **Internet Management**

This international network of linked computer networks is not owned or controlled by any single entity. No person, entity, or government represents the Internet. Order is maintained by voluntary, non-profit membership working groups, including the Internet Society (ISOC), established in 1992 to develop standards, maintain routing tables, allocate addresses, and promote global information exchange. The major costs of operating the Internet are borne by its principal users, universities, research laboratories, corporations, and foreign governments which pay for the part of the system they use.

Internet demographics reflect the volatility of the Net. It is estimated that the Internet is doubling every year, with about 20 million users currently. Other estimates are higher, up to about 30 million users.

■ **Interoperability**

The Internet provides interoperability, which means that computers running on different operating systems and software that ordinarily are incompatible, can run compatibly when internetworked. Other computer networks, such as those run commercially by CompuServe, America On Line, and Prodigy, offer their subscribers access to the Internet, but technically are not part of it.

■ **The World Wide Web**

The Web is a part of the Internet where commercialization is occuring rapidly. It is the focus of growing business and educational interest. The Web was launched in 1992 and by 1993 supported about 100 Web sites. By 1996, this number is expected to surpass 100,000.

The NSF allowed commercialization on the NSFNET beginning in November 1992. The Web surged in popularity in 1993 when Mosaic, a hypermedia (hypertext and multimedia) browser, was introduced. The Web provides an environment for worldwide information retrieval via links based on a hypertext transport protocol (HTTP). This system allows users to point to a link and click on the address. This gives routing information to the system software, which retrieves electronic documents from the clicked-on site. Data are transmitted almost instantaneously, depending on the user's modem or connection speed, and traffic, and may include text documents, pictures, sound, video, 3-D images, and real time live communication.

INTERNET COMMUNICATION

The Internet is a communication channel, like print, traditional broadcast, the telephone, or a facsimile machine, but with some differences. Internet communication can complement a traditional channel, like the telephone, or replace it entirely. It can be conducted in real time with one or more other parties geographically a half world away. Voice e-mail is a telephone equivalent; add video and it becomes an international videophone. Either way, it can be far less expensive and faster than either alternative. The Internet excells at communication and information retrieval. It also is becoming an extremely active marketplace.

Electronic mail (e-mail) is the most commonly-used feature of the Internet. It can be used for:

- Intra-campus and inter-campus communication.
- One sender -to- one receiver communication.
- One sender -to- many receivers communication.
- Many senders -to- many receivers through distribution lists, newsgroups, and bulletin boards.
- Delayed or real time interactive communication using the TALK command.
- Receiving and sending information domestically and internationally[*].

[*] The Internet currently links the United States, Canada, most of South America, Europe (West and East), Russia, Australia, New Zealand, South Africa, Israel, and several countries in North Africa.

The process of communicating electronically requires using addressed data packages that carry a domain address or IP numeric designation. For example, the following is an imaginary unique e-mail address on a university computer.

cbosams@ucc.ku.edu

cbosams = userid

cbo = College of Business

sams = User name, within the 8 letter limit

indicates that the computer address follows

ucc = University Computing Center, the computer

ku = the university paying for the computer

edu = top level domain, educational institution

his could also be written with a 32-bit IP numeric designation address, if it were known, for example 147.54.254.128.

The domain identifies who is supporting the site or addresses. Frequently used domain designations include:

- com   commercial
- edu   educational institution

- gov   government
- mil   military
- net   network
- org   organization
- uk   United Kingdom
- ca   Canada
- au   Australia
- sa   South Africa

In order to send a message to cbosams, most e-mail addresses must be preceeded by an **in%** and enclosed in quotes.

in%"cbosams@ucc.ku.edu"

When using e-mail, you must assume that:

- There is no privacy; any communication can be broken into, so THINK before you speak.
- Some mail bounces (won't get delivered) because it is misaddressed, the addressee's computer host is down, the addressee's mailbox is full, or the Net's computer gremlins were hungry and ate it.
- There are delays, usually unexplained, that can add minutes or even hours to delivery times.
- If you get lots of mail and let it pile up, you will eventually run out of storage space and mail addressed to you will get bounced (not accepted) and sent back to sender.
- Because e-mail is emotionless, you can easily have your feelings hurt or hurt someone else, so read the Netiquette section BEFORE sending e-mail.
- Once you've used it, you'll get hooked on it!

Internet services, for those places that Internet-connect, provide e-mail, along with FTP, Telnet, and navigational enhancements.

- FTP is anonymous File Transport and it links your computer to another at a remote site. This is the primary method for transferring files on the Internet. It allows you to view a public access directory and files, move between directories and files, get a file, and e-mail it back to your mailbox, often at a 14,400 bps transfer speed or higher.
- Telnet is the main Internet protocol for actually connecting with a remote machine.
- Navigational enhancements are services that help you find sites and information on the Internet. Gopher servers at Internet sites provide information about the site in an organized, accessible form. A Gopher server provides a directory with links to other directories and files. Archie is a query system that scans FTP sites, directories, and files.

Usenet is a service where individuals can participate in an exchange of ideas on a particular topic. Over fifteen thousand newsgroups are part of Usenet, which is an abbreviation for "User's Network", a service that makes the Internet available to people for general information exchange.

Not all newsgroups are part of the Internet. Newsgroups, also called (incorrectly) bulletin boards and lists, are mostly hosted by universities and the government. They are organized hierarchially, with seven major categories: comp (computers), misc (miscellaneous), soc (social issues), talk (political and social debates), news (news about networks), rec (hobbies), alt (sex, anarchy, controversy), and biz (business groups). Moderated news groups are administered by a list owner who keeps the discussion focused and maintains control over tempers and behaviors. The moderator can block out a discussant who is disturbing the flow of the list. On an unmoderated group, anything goes, and often does.

NETIQUETTE

You've probably heard how anarchy reigns on the Internet. While this is true to an extent and individuality is highly esteemed, you must also be aware that Victorian-like rules of proper conduct also prevail. This is commonly called Netiquette. If you join a newsgroup, it's wise to "lurk" and learn how the group works before contributing. Newsgroups usually post FAQs (Frequently Asked Questions) that describe the particular Netiquette of the group. Some other suggestions include

- When you communicate on the Internet, NEVER USE ALL UPPER CASE LETTERS BECAUSE THIS MEANS YOU ARE SHOUTING! In fact, the vast majority of communication is conducted in the far calmer environment of lower case letters. If you shout, you may become the recipient of a

- FLAME! Because the Internet is semi-anonymous, we identify one another by name, but there is no absolute guarantee that someone is who he/she claims, people sometimes lose their inhibitions and send very abrupt, nasty, and upsetting messages to others. This is called a flame. When flames start flying between people, it is called a FLAME WAR.

- Don't use profanity on the Internet, particularly in moderated lists which forbid it as a means of maintaining order, civility, and some control over members' tempers.

- People are working on the Internet, so professional behavior and responsible conduct are expected.

- Don't blather, send multiple e-mail pages of verbiage but never get to the point; spew, feel that you have to comment on everything;, or spam, send unwanted messages to vast numbers of people.

- In replying to something that is posted on a list, identify the thread to which you are responding. For example,
  Re: White Castle Hamburger—this is the thread

- Because e-mail is emotionless, sarcasm and humor often are misunderstood. To humanize the message, many people use acronyms and smileys, but don't overdo them! The list of acronyms and emoticons grows daily. Some examples are:

■ Acronym Dictionary

- BTW   By the way
- DVF   Ducking very fast
- FAQ   Frequently Asked Questions
- FWIW   For what it's worth
- FYI   For your information
- FUA   Frequently used acronyms
- IMO   In my opinion
- IMHO   In my humble opinion
- IOW   In other words
- NRN   No reply necessary
- OTOH   On the other hand
- ROFL   Rolling on the floor laughing
- TIA   Thanks in advance
- TIC   Tongue in cheek
- TCITM   The check's in the mail

- ■ **"Smileys" (Emoticons)**

  - :-)   Standard smiley face (read with head on left shoulder)
  - :-(Frowning face
  - ;-)   Wink
  - :-D   Laughing
  - :-/   Sceptical
  - :-X   Lips are sealed
  - :-   Making a very biting, sarcastic remark
  - %-)   Been staring at a computer screen too long
  - :-~(Have a cold
  - :-&   Am tongue tied
  - -O   Tired, yawning

GETTING STARTED

Because changes occur daily on the Internet and World Wide Web, no address or citation can be guaranteed past the publication date of this *Study Guide*. These sites provide useful information or are just interesting places to visit. The addresses are case sensitive, which means that everything is lower case UNLESS it is capitalized, in which case you MUST use caps in the address.

- ■ **Search Engines And Navigators**

  Yahoo at Stanford University
  http://www.yahoo.com
  WebCrawler (tm)
  http://webcrawler.com
  World Wide Web Worm (WWWW)
  http://www.cs.colorado.edu/home/mcbryan/WWWW.html
  World Internet Catalog
  http://nearnet.gnn.com
  Lycos at Carnegie Mellon University
  http://lycos.cs.cmu.edu

- ■ **General Interest**

  "Big Dummies Guide to the Internet"
  http://www.nova.edu/Inter-Links/bigdummy/bdg_toc.html
  SBA On-Line
  http://www.sbaonline.sba.gov
  Fedworld - U.S. Government Home Page
  http://www.fedworld.gov
  Census Information
  http://www.census.gov

Library of Congress
http://lcweb.loc.gov
CIA World Factbook
http://www.odci.gov
European Union
http://www.echo.lu
http://www.undcp.or.at/unlinks.html
World Bank
http://www.worldbank.org

LAUNCHING YOUR CAREER

MARKETING YOURSELF TO PROSPECTIVE EMPLOYERS

A career begins with a first job. Whether you are a traditional student seeking a first, entry-level marketing job or a non-traditional student seeking a first job after a career change, you must take responsibility for your job search, organize and direct your job search efforts, and commit to stick with the process until you find the marketing job that is right for you. Set goals for yourself at each step of the search process and give yourself sufficient time to accomplish them. Use all available job search resources and particularly your school's career planning office.

■ Develop The Skills That Employers Value

Although it is impossible to identify the skills valued by each marketing employer, some skills generally are highly valued, regardless of marketing job type. These include:

- Communication skills — writing and speaking fluently, expressing your thoughts accurately and concisely, and listening carefully.
- Learning skills — pursuing lifetime and job-specific learning, and educational attainment.
- Information skills — skillfully using modern tools and technologies to identify information needs and resources, retrieve information, and use it in making sound marketing decisions.
- People skills — knowing how to interact effectively with customers, work productively on teams, negotiate, and be flexible in developing collaborative solutions to marketing problems.
- Creativity skills — seeking new ways to solve old problems and unexpected paths to achieve organizational success, avoiding habitual responses to situations that demand unique reactions.
- Motivation skills — willingly taking the initiative, encouraging others to do so, accepting leadership responsibilities, and sticking with a task until it is successfully completed.

EXPLORING MARKETING CAREERS

As most students near graduation, they feel relief that this phase of their education is almost complete, and reservations, if not outright fear, about what lies ahead in the job market. While students may learn their class lessons well, rarely are they equally well educated about how to explore career and job opportunities and market themselves to prospective employers.

Most students wait until their last term to begin thinking about what they will do after graduation. They frequently have unrealistic expectations about careers and jobs, which can lead to disappointment. What can a student do to explore marketing careers and target interesting and promising job types?

- The first step is to get to know yourself. In the following sections you will have an opportunity to perform two types of self-assessments designed to identify your job-related strengths and weaknesses and the benefits you can offer a prospective employer. It is important to develop an objective profile of yourself. This will help you make a match with a career that fits your skills, abilities, and interests.
- The second step is to find out more about marketing careers and the jobs associated with different career paths. This research can be performed in several different ways.

Using hardcopy resources. Most school and public libraries have career guides in their reference areas, both books and periodicals. Your school career center also will have information on many different careers, including marketing. You can contact some of the career resources listed at the end of this section and request information on careers. Ask these organizations if they have a local professional association chapter. If they do, students often can attend chapter meetings at a reduced rate or at no charge. Attending progessional meetings is a good way to learn about a career and the people whose jobs you find most interesting.

Internet sources. Many career resources are on the Internet. You can access them using a search engine or navigational guide identified in the Internet section of this *Study Guide*. You will find Department of Labor and Department of Commerce information on employment trends on the Internet. Career and job search tools are available at various university sites. A growing number of Internet companies will help you write a resume and list it on the Internet, for a fee.

Hands-on research. If you prefer a more hands-on approach, you can investigate marketing careers by participating in a shadowing program or an internship. Many school career centers operate shadowing programs where students spend a day "shadowing" a professional and learning about their job. In marketing, this might involve shadowing an advertising account executive, a brand manager, a retail store manager, or a salesperson. Alternately, many students are signing up for internships and co-operative programs where they work part-time in a business while attending school. In both cases, shadowing and internships/co-ops, students get a close look at what marketing jobs are like from an employee's perspective.

Visiting career and job fairs. Many schools plan career and job fairs for their students. This is usually a one-day trade fair where representatives from businesses, organizations, and professional groups are invited to set up tables with displays and printed materials, and meet with students interested in researching career and job opportunities. If your school doesn't sponsor such a fair, another school in the area may. Often several schools will pool resources and jointly sponsor such an event.

- Once you have narrowed down your career and job choices, the next step is to begin to look at opportunities in specific businesses and organizations. Research the companies that interest you, find out as much as possible about their business and the industry in which they operate. Some of this information is in the library; an increasing volume of company information can be found on the Internet, both at company home page sites and in data bases, such as the EDGAR site, a repository of Securities and Exchange (SEC) filings. Organize the information you collect into files for each company you have targeted.

- Once you have identified employment targets, the next step is to begin making contacts, sending out resumes, and scheduling interviews.

ASSESSING YOUR EMPLOYABILITY

It is important to begin any job search by assessing your job-related strengths and weaknesses so you can determine if you are a good match with a particular job's specifications. You should also clearly understand what you are seeking in a job, the opportunities you can take advantage of in learning about job availability, and the threats to getting the job you want.

Remember the S-W and O-T Grids from PART I: Becoming a Better Student? The same process, an adapted SWOT Analysis, can be used to develop a job-related profile for your job search. Use the grids on the following pages to perform a self-analysis of the strengths and weaknesses you bring to a job search, and the opportunities and threats that you face in the process. This exercise is designed for your eyes alone, so be honest with yourself as you complete the grids.

In the "My Job Strengths" cell, list all the job strengths that you possess. Evaluate your strengths very broadly. For example, consider what employers value, such as:

- communication skills
- learning and education
- information retrieval skills
- management skills

26

- ability to work with other people
- creativity
- motivation

Also consider your work experience, internships, and co-ops; organizational skills; recreational interests; life experiences; computer knowledge; marketing courses completed; willingness to relocate; memory; sensititivty to others; and work attitudes. Once your list is complete, rank order it with the strength(s) that employers value most ranked number one.

When it comes to job weaknesses, be honest in assessing your deficiencies. List every weakness that may undermine your ability to get the job you want. For example, you may have poor computer or mathematical skills, can't type very well, and dislike speaking in front of groups. List your weaknesses, rank order them (worst one(s) from an employer's perspective ranked number one), then consider taking steps to reduce or eliminate them as weaknesses. In this case, some reasonable corrective steps include taking a computer class, enrolling in a math refresher, learning to type, and taking a public speaking course. Set self-improvement goals that will convert your weaknesses to strengths.

In the Opportunities cell, list every person and organization that can help you in the job search process by providing information, references, advice, or contacts. For example, you may learn of job opportunities from family and friends. You can get career guidance from your school's career center. The school library and the Internet have references that describe careers and provide information about job trends. You can get assistance from previous employers, school alumni, members of professional and community organizations. Make your list as broad as possible; consider all possible sources that can broaden your exposure to job openings and career choices.

Finally, under Threats, realistically list every possible threat to your getting the job you want. For example, a considerable threat is the competition, other people with more experience and education applying for the same jobs. Survey the general employment picture and determine if national employment trends are working for or against you. Is the economy in your area and the nation robust or declining? You will be unable to change the macro-level threats. However, you should know about them and consider what defensive actions you can take. For example, if employment opportunities are projected to decline in one career area, expand your search to include careers where jobs are expected to grow and you also have interests and strengths. For those threats that you can change, set goals for doing so.

S-W GRID

My Job Strengths	My Job Weaknesses

O-T GRID

My Opportunities	Threats

IDENTIFYING HOW YOU'LL BENEFIT AN EMPLOYER

The Features-Advantages-Benefits (FAB) method is a widely used selling technique that identifies customer needs, then shows how product features are advantages that benefit the customer. The three FAB factors must be used together, for alone they lose considerable power in facilitating an exchange.

Product <u>features</u> include physical characteristics and performance capabilities, such things as product size, shape, uses, costs, and performance dimensions. An <u>advantage</u> describes how the product can be used to help the customer. A <u>benefit</u> is the favorable outcome the customer will experience from the product. FAB uniquely and specifically relates a product's features and advantages to customer benefits. One product usually has multiple features, all of which can serve customer needs.

FAB answers the question, "What's in it for me?" This is a need-satisfying approach that focuses on the customer's self-interest. In the student - prospective employer context, FAB identifies student features as advantages that can benefit the employer. Thus, the student is the product and the employer is the customer.

A model of FAB adapted for students is shown on the next page. Step 1 is as critical for students as it is for salespeople; both must determine what the customer <u>needs</u>. In the case of the employer, needs are the job requirements of the vacant position. Looking at it another way, the needs are also problems the new hire is expected to solve. Employer needs should be listed in priority order, beginning with the most important. Step 2 matches each need with a particular student <u>feature</u> (skill, ability, personality characteristic, educational attainment). In Step 3, the needs and features are arrayed in a FAB Matrix and become information points which are used to construct a cover letter, resume, or interview presentation in Step 4.

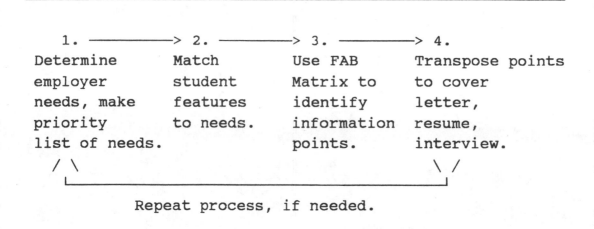

```
                    FAB for Students
_____

     1. ─────────> 2. ─────────> 3. ─────────> 4.
  Determine        Match         Use FAB       Transpose points
  employer         student       Matrix to     to cover
  needs, make      features      identify      letter,
  priority         to needs.     information   resume,
  list of needs.                 points.       interview.
     / \                                          \ /
     └─────────────────────────────────────────────┘

           Repeat process, if needed.

_____
```

The job-seeking marketing student must approach a prospective employer with knowledge of the employer's job <u>needs</u> as well as her own job-related <u>features</u>. Needs and features are systematically matched in the FAB Matrix (next page). In Column A of the Matrix, the student identifies what the job requires (skills, abilities, training, etc.) in order to satisfy the employer's needs. In Column B, student features are matched to the needs. Column C states the feature's advantage. Column D states the benefit to

Students can obtain information on what an employer needs (i.e., the job requires) by asking the company's personnel office for a job description, interviewing current company employees, observing the company's employees, asking faculty or your school's career center about the company, or "shadowing" a company manager for a day.

Carefully examine the Fab Matrix on the next page, then try your hand at the practice FAB matrix, matching your strengths to a fictional employer's needs. With practice, a FAB matrix exercise can become a valuable part of your job search activities. Working through the FAB process helps focus your attention on strengths that will benefit an employer. It emphasizes the goodness-of-fit between your product features and the job's requirements, which can be a powerful advantage when you write your cover letter and resume, and prepare for screening and selection interviews.

In the following example, assume that you contacted the company advertising the job to ask for a job description. From the description you have identified key job needs as (1) good skills in individual and group communications; (2) using a laptop computer for database, word processing, and spreadsheet applications; and (3) the ability to telecommute.

The FAB Matrix

	A Employer NEED or Problem: "This job requires..."	B Student FEATURE: "I have..."	C ADVANTAGE: "This means...	D Employer BENEFIT: "You will..."
1.	good skills in individual and group communication	been debate club member for 5 years, made presen- tations in five classes	I require little training because I have exp- erience and confidence	save on training cost and time, training; I can begin work almost immediately
2.	using laptop computer for database, word processing, spreadsheets	used a lap- top for 3 years, know software applications	I can begin using a Lap- top and the programs very quickly	save training time and money; reduce initial errors because I am experienced
3.	some telecommuting required	telecommuted part-time in a co-op, telemarketing at home and the office	I know how to work at home productively	benefit because I have already learned how to work at home, won't waste time getting organized
4.	....			

Now that you have seen how FAB works, try your hand at a sample FAB. In this case, assume that you are working from a job description obtained from the company. The employer needs someone who has experience in:

- information search and retrieval
- report writing skills
- the ability to work alone, in small teams and in groups
- is dependable, motivated, and able to take responsibility

Use the space provided to identify features that relate to each of these needs. For example, consider classes where you have used the library to search for and retrieve information, or your marketing class if you use the Internet to retrieve information. You may have work experience that matches this need, perhaps from a previous employer who had you reading trade journals or collecting information from a federal government source. When you state the advantage, relate your product features to the need. In the benefit column, take the employer's perspective and identify precisely how hiring you can satisfy the need and provide a substantial benefit to the employer.

A Sample FAB Matrix

A Employer NEED or Problem:	B Student FEATURE:	C ADVANTAGE:	D Employer BENEFIT:
"This job requires..."	"I have..."	"This means...	"You will..."
1. experience in information search and retrieval			
2. report writing skills			
3. ability to work alone, in small teams and in groups			
4. dependable, motivated, able to take responsibility			

YOUR OWN MARKETING PLAN

If you aspire to enter or advance in marketing, you should think of the process in terms of marketing yourself; developing a plan for finding a good match between your skills, abilities, experiences, and interests, and an appropriate marketing job that leads in the long-term to a rewarding career. If you invest in developing your own marketing plan, it will give you valuable practice in writing a plan, and help you focus on what must be accomplished in the process of identifying a target career and job types. This is not a process to be undertaken lightly. In order for it to provide useful guidance, you must work through each section of the marketing plan diligently and completely.

It would be impractical to provide space for a complete marketing plan in this *Study Guide* because a thorough marketing plan could run to 50, 60, or a hundred pages or more. Instead, each marketing plan section is identified and the type of information needed is described. It is up to you to fill in the blanks.

Your Name _____

Date _____

I. Executive Summary

This is a 1 to 2 page summary that includes key points from each section and provides an overview of the high points of the plan. Write the Executive Summary last, after you have developed your plan and can summarize it fluently. It will serve as a reminder of what you've written in the complete plan.

II. Situation Analysis

This section provides a detailed analysis of the factors that will influence your success in marketing yourself to prospective employers. It includes information about the industry and the three or four companies that you're most interested in, along with an analysis of yourself (the product) and the market, including competition. Information about yourself (the product) can be taken directly from your SWOT and FAB analyses, as well as academic records, personal files, and job references. Industry and company information will be found in government documents, industry and trade journals, industry and company reports, articles in the current popular business press, and many sources on the Internet. This section should contain an:

A. Industry analysis including employment trends, growth forecasts, demand patterns, and job types in the target industry where you are most interested in working, for example, in retail, wholesale, promotion, product developing, personal selling, agricultural marketing, or health care marketing.

B. Company analysis for each of the three or four businesses where you would most like to work, including their history, mission, current employment situation, projected growth, core competencies, strengths and weaknesses, hiring practices, names and addresses for obtaining employment forms, and contacts.

C. Product analysis including the results of your personal SWOT and FAB, as well as a summary of your academic background, relevant courses completed, job experiences, professional interests, organizational memberships, job location preferences, value you can bring to a job, and a thoughtful analysis of what you want and expect from a job.

D. Market analysis of occupational forecasts from such sources as the Department of Labor and Department of Commerce, found in libraries and on the Internet.

E. Competitive analysis including characteristics of others who may be competing for the same jobs, both entry-level applicants and applicants with experience, their relative strengths and weaknesses. A competitive analysis should also look at the target company's competition. This information may prove particularly useful in a selection interview if the interviewer asks what you think about his company's competition. Knowledge about the company and its competition shows the intensity of your interest in working for the company.

F. Analysis of other environmental factors that may affect your job search including economic forecasts, political outlook, technological advances, relevant social forces.

III. Marketing Objectives

This section provides a broad statement of the objectives set for marketing to accomplish in your job search. You should:

A. Identify priority objectives to be satisfied, time frames for achieving objectives, time limits by which specific job search activities should be completed. For example, a top objective is to research the industry and target companies. If you work on this over the school year, it may take several months or more to obtain the necessary information. Set a realistic time limit and state it in the plan.

B. Objectively specify your goals for resumes mailed, job contacts made, interviews completed, job offers received, or other quantifiable measures. Consider the amount of work that must be completed before you can begin to work on resumes, contacts, and interviews. Then identify your goals and approximately how long they will take to accomplish. This should give you a realistic vision of the complexity of this process and the time required.

C. Specify other objectives, for example establishing a network of contacts, learning about job opportunities, or how to conduct a job search.

IV. Marketing Strategies

This section makes a statement about how marketing will help you achieve the objectives and goals set for your job search. It is easier to write if you work from representative job specifications, which can be obtained from a school career center, library, newspaper and trade journal job listings, and companies. You should:

A. State the general marketing strategies for positioning (making a prospective employer aware of your value compared to other job applicants), and your competitive advantage. Use your SWOT and FAB analyses in this section.

B. State specific marketing strategies, particularly for gathering needed information, obtaining necessary assistance from others, obtaining employment forms, making contacts, arranging interviews.

V. Tactics

This section provides a statement of how the strategies will be implemented, including plans for each of the marketing mix elements. You should:

A. Identify tactical responsibilities, how others may assist in your job search including employment contacts, job and character references, your school's career office personnel who can help you develop job search and interview skills, professional employment agencies, resources for conducting Internet job searches.

B. State product tactics including improving necessary job and interview skills, correcting job-related weaknesses, selecting appropriate clothing to wear to a job interview.

C. Identify price tactics for salary and benefits, including statements of price points from introductory pricing (lowest beginning salary) to mid- and top salary expectations, price adjustments (when you would reasonably expect to receive increases), and benefits including vacations, health, dental, retirement, profit-sharing plans.

D. Identify place tactics including if and where you are willing to relocate, whether or not you are willing to travel (some, moderately, extensively) on the job.

E. Provide promotion tactics including plans for producing hardcopy and electronic resumes, development of employer mailing lists, identification of employment bulletin boards addresses on the Internet, and newspaper classified advertisement sections.

VI. Budget

This section states how your job-search budget will be allocated with associated costs. Job searching can be expensive in time, effort, and monetary terms. It is helpful to be able to estimate your costs so you can plan ahead and allocate the resources that will be needed. You should:

A. Provide a detailed analysis of costs including those associated with resume production and distribution, interviewing, travel and clothing costs, postage, telephone, and electronic expenses.

B. Provide a breakout of allocations for how the budget will be spent to cover costs and market the product.

VII. Control

This section provides a detailed description of how the marketing plan will be evaluated by outcome measures, including call-back interviews and job offers; benchmarks and time frames should be provided, along with the construction of a time line that identifies key time periods when objectives should be accomplished.

VIII. Appendices

At the end of the marketing plan, include additional materials that support various parts of the plan, including transcripts, letters of recommendation from teachers or previous employers, a portfolio of your best class work, industry reports, articles on job search skills, and lists of contact names and addresses.

A portfolio is a collection of samples of your best work. Many students are asked during an interview if they have samples of their work to show, which illustrates the wisdom of compiling a portfolio. Your portfolio can include:

- class reports, that demonstrate your information retrieval, analytical, and writing skills
- simulations, where you have taken part in a series of decisions based on real world marketing problems
- promotion plans, where you have developed a promotion plan and campaign for a particular product or brand
- Internet home page designs, that display your creativity and consumer insight
- marketing research, where you have worked successfully in a team or small group
- quantitative analyses and spreadsheets, that display your organizational and mathematical skills
- computer generated reports, that show your ability to use a word processor and graphical display programs

Be sure that any work included in a portfolio is your best. Check spelling and grammar, remove mistakes, and be sure that the work is clean, neat, and well organized.

WRITING A RESUME

A cover letter and resume are the first contact most businesses have with a job applicant. Some businesses receive hundreds of resumes each week, most get filed or discarded. Some corporations electronically scan resumes, input the data to a program that allows a key word search, then search the entire resume data bank when a vacancy occurs to match job needs with applicant features.

A cover letter must be clean, neat, well organized, and without grammar, spelling, or typographical errors. It should provide carefully selected information tailored to the job. A cover letter addressed to the person (by name) directing the job search must accompany each resume. In it you should:

- Identify the position for which you are applying.
- State concisely why you are qualified for the position and refer the reader to your enclosed resume where details are listed.

- Ask for an interview.
- Provide information about how, where, and when you can be reached.

The resume should be:

- Clear, simple, and concise. Typically one page for a new graduate with little experience and more pages for job and career changers.
- In a readable font, such as Times 10 point type. Some style variations such as boldface, italics, and underline can be used. The resume should be printed on a white or neutral bond paper, computer typed, laser printed, and carefully spell checked and edited.
- Complete, with sufficient information so the applicant screener can see at a glance that you have the qualifications needed to justify a screening interview. Be honest, never lie, but exercise care in providing information that could hurt you.
- Organized, with standard resume information sections, including:
    - <u>Identification</u>—provide your name, address, city, state, zip code, phone, fax number. This information is usually centered at the top of the first page and in bold type.
    - <u>Career objective statement</u>—what you are seeking in a career that matches with the job for which you're applying.
    - <u>Work experience</u>—in reverse chronological order, with most current job listed first. This can include internships and co-ops.
    - <u>Education</u>—with your last degree listed first, including dates, name of school, location. This section may also include relevant coursework.
    - <u>Extracurricular activities</u>—particularly those activities that demonstrate your job-related interests, evidence of leadership, motivation, and assuming responsibility for others.
    - <u>Skills, strengths</u> that are relevant to the job.
    - <u>Personal information</u> (optional).
    - <u>References</u>, either available on request or listed.

Resumes can be posted on the Internet. To investigate the possibilities, use a search engine or navigational guide to locate career resources, or search target company home pages to determine if they accept resumes electronically. As with all Internet activities, proceed with caution. Check any fee-based resume service carefully before you list with them.

DEVELOPING INTERVIEWING SKILLS

Most people are apprehensive about job interviews. An interview can be a highly stressful process, sometimes made more stressful by interviewers who deliberately ask unexpected and unnerving questions. While the job interview is an important process for evaluating applicants, surprisingly few applicants make a serious enough effort to prepare for it.

A typical job applicant participates first in a screening interview designed to screen out applicants who are obviously unsuited to the job. This type of interview is conducted by a trained interviewer who evaluates job-related strengths along with the applicant's appearance, grammar, body language, confidence, and ability to handle stressful situations. The interview begins with introductions and probing questions designed to verify resume information. Some assessment questions are asked, often followed by a period of silence, to test the applicant's reactions, or a broad question such as "What can you tell me about yourself?", which may leave the ill prepared applicant struggling for words or lead to a babble of poorly connected thoughts. The session winds up with several closing questions. Afterward the interviewer evaluates the applicant's performance and determines whether the applicant will continue in the process or be dropped from further consideration. Some tips for screening interviews include:

- Wear appropriate clothing, avoid faddish or extreme styles, stick with conservative suits and business clothes.
- Be early to the interview and never late.
- If the interview room door is closed, knock before entering.
- Come into the interview room with a confident stride.
- Make eye contact with the interviewer, greet the person by name, and give a firm but appropriate hand shake.
- When the interviewer motions you to a chair, position yourself so you can make eye contact with the interviewer.
- Never slouch in the chair, draw it close to the interviewer's desk, or prop yourself in the chair and rest your arms on the desk.
- Don't sit hunched forward or with your legs awkwardly crossed.
- Never bite your fingernails, chew gum, crack your knuckles, drum your fingers on the chair arm, tap your feet, or engage in other distracting mannerisms.
- Relax, listen carefully to the interviewer's questions, and think before you answer.
- Be courteous.
- Smile.
- Never use profanities.
- Tell the truth.
- At the conclusion of the interview, thank the interviewer for taking the time to interview you, shake hands, and leave.

The next step is one or more selection interviews. Selection interviews often are conducted on-site, where the job is located and with actual supervisors and peers. While the screening interview determines if the applicant has the ability, training, skill, and interest to do the job, selection interviews try to find out if the applicant is the right person for the job and will fit the company's culture. Questions in screening interviews are designed to reveal what the applicant is like as a person. Many questions may be asked, including

- How will you fit in with this organization?
- What are your goals?
- Why do you want this job?
- What can you do for the company?
- What do you think of our products?
- What do you think of our competition?
- Why do you want to work for this company?
- What subjects did you like most in school?
- What subjects did you like least in school?
- What do you like to do with your free time?
- Do you have any hobbies?
- What activities give you the most satisfaction?

At some point during the selection process, the applicant has a chance to ask questions. This provides the applicant with an opportunity to show evidence of preparation and thoughtfulness. Some questions that might be asked, if they haven't already been answered, include

- What would a typical work day be like for someone in this job?
- What training can I expect? Is it formal or on-the-job?

- Do others in my position hold the _____ degree?
- What is the career path for someone in this job?
- Does the company tend to promote from within or look for outside hires to fill upper level jobs?
- Does the company offer educational support if I decided to pursue a higher degree?
- Is travel expected of someone in this job? Is it domestic or also international?
- What are the chances that I'll be asked to relocate?
- What benefits come with the job, including health, dental, life insurance, etc.
- Could you describe the work environment? Where will I be working and with whom?
- When can I expect to hear whether I've gotten the job?

Be prepared to discuss salary, although that often is not brought up until after an applicant has been offered the job. You may be asked about your salary expectations. Be prepared to respond to the question. Some jobs include a salary range with the job description; others may use the phrase "competitive salary" offered. Your research should uncover the range of salaries usually associated with the job type; just be sure that you factor in local living costs since they vary and can affect your ability to live on a base salary.

A school career center often can help prepare you for an interview by conducting a mock interview. This process simulates a screening interview and often is taped so you can play it back and critique your performance. If you can't participate in a mock interview, ask a friend who has participated in job interviews to role play with you, as the applicant. Think ahead to how you will handle your part of the interview and be prepared.

CAREER RESOURCES

Some professional organizations that may be helpful in providing specialized marketing career information are listed in this section. While every effort has been made to provide the most current information organizations, like individuals, can and do move. If you have difficulty locating a forwarding address, try a library search of telephone directories or a directory of professional organizations. In the next several years, as more professional organizations set up sites on the World Wide Web, you will be able to find them through an Internet search using any of the public search tools. Internet addresses are provided for organizations that could be located on the Internet in mid-1995.

■ **Organizations**

Advertising Council

261 Madison Avenue
New York, NY 10016-2303
212-922-1500

American Advertising Federation

1101 Vermont Ave. N.W., Suite 500
Washington, DC 20005
202-898-0089

American Association of Advertising Agencies

666 3rd Avenue, 13th Floor
New York, NY 10017-4056
212-682-2500
http://www.commercepark.com/AAAA/AAAA.html

American Marketing Association

250 S. Wacker Drive, Suite 200
Chicago, IL 60606-5819
312-648-0536
1-800-262-1150
http://www.nsns.com/MouseTracks

Association of Industry Manufacturers Representatives

222 Merchandise Mart Plaza
Chicago, IL 60654
312-464-0092

Bank Marketing Association

1120 Connecticut Avenue, N.W.
Washington, DC 20036
202-663-5268

Direct Marketing Association

11 West 42nd Street
New York, NY 10036-8096
212-768-7277

Direct Selling Education Foundation

1776 K Street, N.W., Suite 600
Washington, DC 20006
202-293-5760

Food Marketing Institute

800 Connecticut Avenue, N.W., Suite 500
Washington, DC 20006-2701
202-452-8444

International Advertising Association

342 Madison Ave., 20th Floor, Suite 2000
New York, NY 10173-0073
212-557-1133

International Association of Sales Professionals

13 East 37th Street
New York, NY 10016
212-683-9755

Manufacturers' Agents National Association

23016 Mill Creek Road
P.O. Box 3467
Laguna Hills, CA 92654
714-859-4040

National Association for Professional Saleswomen

1730 N. Lynn Street, Suite 502
Arlington, VA 22209
1-800-823-6277

National Association of Real Estate Brokers

1629 K Street, N.W., Suite 306
Washington, DC 20006
202-785-4477

National Association of Realtors

430 N. Michigan Avenue
Chicago, IL 60611-4087
312-329-8200

National Association of Wholesalers-Distributors

1725 K Street, N.W.
Washington, DC 10006
202-872-0885

National Retail Federation

701 Pennsylvania Avenue, N.W.
Washington, DC 20004
202- 783-7971

Outdoor Advertising Association of America

1850 M St., Suite 1040
Washington, DC 20036
202-833-5566

Point-of-Purchase Advertising Institute

66 N. Van Brunt St.
Englewood, NJ 07631
201-894-8899

Promotional Products Association International

3125 Skyway Circle N.
Irving, TX 75038-3526
214-252-0404

Public Relations Society of America

33 Irving Place, 3rd Floor
New York, NY 10003-2376
212-995-2230
http://www.prsa.org

Retail Advertising and Marketing Association International

500 N. Michigan Avenue, Suite 600
Chicago, IL 60611
312-245-9011

Sales and Marketing Executives International

Statler Office Tower
Cleveland, OH 44115
1-800-999-1414

■ References

Ayre, Rick and Don Willmott (1995), "The Internet Means Business," *PC Magazine* (May 16): 195-200.

Bliss, Edwin C. (1976), Getting Things Done, New York: Scribner and Sons, Inc.

Brown, Alex and Richard Gordon (1994), "Demystifying the Internet," University of Delaware (August), http://www.udel.edu/aamsler/mba/mbapage1.html.

Butler, Grady L. and Daniel R. Boyd (1988), "Successful Interviewing," *Journal of Education for Business* (March): 282-284.

Cost, Doris L., Marcia H. Bishop, and Elizabeth Scott Anderson (1992), "Effective Listening: Teaching Students a Critical Marketing Skill," *Journal of Marketing Education* (Spring): 41-45.

Douglass, Merill E. and Donna N. Douglass (1980), Manage Your Time, Manage Your Work, Manage Yourself, New York: Amacom.

Ellis, David B. (1984), Becoming a Master Student, Rapid City,   SD: College Survival, Inc.

Elmer-DeWitt, Philip (1993), "First Nation in Cyberspace," *Time* (December 6): 62-54, posted to interesting-people@eff.org.

Garrison, Lloyd L. (1984), "Communicating - The Nonverbal Way," *Journal of Business Education* (February): 190-192.

Horn, J. Kenneth (1986), "Giving the Prospective Employer the 'Inner View' in One's Job Search," *Journal of Business Education* (March): 249-251.

Kehoe, Brendan P. (1992), Zen and the Art of the Internet: A Beginner's Guide to the Internet, First Edition, by electronic file transfer (FTP) from INET_ZEN.TXT, Chester, PA: Widener University.

Kelley, Craig A. (1992), "Educating Marketing Students in the Art of Business Etiquette," *Journal of Marketing Education* (Summer): 34-39.

Krol, Ed and Ellen Hoffman (1993), "FYI On 'What Is The Internet?'", from Krol, Ed (1992), The Whole Internet User's Guide and Catalog, Sebastopol, CA: O'Reilly & Associates.

Locke, Edwin A. and Gary P. Latham (1990), A Theory of Goal Setting and Task Performance, Englewood Cliffs, New Jersey: Prentice Hall.

Luke, Robert H. (1989), Business Careers, Boston: Houghton Mifflin Co.: Chapter 5: Marketing, 151-210.

McCorkle, Denny E., Joe F. Alexander, and Memo F. Diriker (1992), "Developing Self-marketing Skills for Student Career Success," *Journal of Marketing Education* (Spring): 57-67.

Mackenzie, Alec (1989), Time for Success: A Goal Getter's Strategy, New York: McGraw-Hill.

Nunez, Annette, V. and Fran Norwood (1985), "Survival Tips for Those Who Take and Give Notes," *Journal of Education for Business* (December): 132-135.

Quarterman, John S. (1994), "Preliminary Partial Results of the Second TIC/MIDS Internet Demographic Survey," Matrix News (December 1994), by electronic file transfer (FTP) from mids@tic.com, http://www.tic.com.

Tec, Leon (1983), Targets: How to Set Goals for Yourself and Reach Them, New York: New American Library.

Thompson, Kenneth N. and Dongdae Lee (1991), "Developing Effective Note-taking Guides for Use in Mass Lecture Sections," *Journal of Marketing Education* (Fall): 40-51.

Sanford, Clive G. (1995), Exploring the Internet, Chicago: Richard D. Irwin, Co.

Schwartz, Carol A. and Rebecca L. Turner, Editors (1995), The Encyclopedia of Associations, 29th Edition, Detroit: Gale Research, Inc.

Shermach, Kelly (1995), "Business Marketers Are Heavy Users of Interactive Catalogs," *Marketing News*, January:15.

Siegel, C. and R. Powers (1991), "FAB: A Useful Technique for the Job-Seeking Marketing Student," *Marketing Education Review*, (Winter): 60-64

Solomon, Stephen D. (1994), "Staking A Claim On The Internet,"   *INC. Technology*: 87-92.

Stair, Lila B. (1995), Careers in Marketing, Lincolnwood, IL: VGM Career Horizons, NTC Publishing Group.

Verity, John W. and Robert D. Hof (1994), "The Internet: How It Will Change The Way You Do Business," *Business Week*, November 14: 80-88.

PART II
MASTERING MARKETING: CHAPTER STUDY GUIDES

Chapter Summary

Chapter Objectives

Chapter Outline

Key Terms

Chapter Questions And Activities

Test Yourself

CHAPTER 1

AN INTRODUCTION TO MARKETING

CHAPTER SUMMARY

Chapter 1 begins your study of marketing with an introduction to marketing as an essential economic activity, as well as a field of study. Some of the most important foundation concepts in marketing are defined. Several convincing reasons for studying marketing are identified and explained. Marketing began with simple barter. Its evolution is traced through American history and the effects of major events such as the Industrial Revolution, the Great Depression, and World War II are noted. The chapter concludes by introducing the marketing mix variables and discussing how product, price, place, and promotion contribute to consumer satisfaction and the achievement of organizational goals. The Chapter 1 opening question is: What would *your* life be like if there were no marketing?

CHAPTER OBJECTIVES

Chapter 1, like all the text chapters, is organized around a series of numbered learning objectives. Each of the five chapter objectives is stated beginning on the next page. Blank space is provided after each statement for you to rewrite the statement as a question, then answer the question in your own words based on what you have read in the corresponding textbook section. By restating the objective statement as a question, it becomes easier to write a concise answer that also summarizes the text section.

The first objective is completed for you, as an example.

Step 1   Restate the objective statement as a question.

Step 2   Read the corresponding section in the textbook.

Step 3   Based on what you have read, answer the objective question.

■ **CHAPTER OBJECTIVES**

1. Define *marketing* and explain its origins and contemporary meanings.

Question: What is marketing? What are its origins and contemporary meanings?

Answer: Marketing is a process of planning, developing, pricing, promoting, and distributing products (goods, services, and ideas) to create exchanges that satisfy individuals and organizations. It is performed by individuals and many different types of organizations, businesses, and governments. In a business, marketing generates revenues and profits. Its origins are in barter. Today, marketing is a highly sophisticated activity designed to fill gaps in the marketplace and add value to exchanges with consumers.

2. Identify the key foundation concepts of marketing.

Question

Answer

3. Explain why it is important to study marketing.

Question

Answer

4. Discuss how and why marketing is evolving.

Question

Answer

5. Describe how marketers use the marketing mix variables to satisfy consumers and achieve organizational goals.

Question

Answer

CHAPTER OUTLINE

Complete this **Chapter Outline** by writing the most important thoughts in each section. For example, begin with Chapter Objective 1. As you read the corresponding section in the textbook and identify an important thought, write a concise statement of that thought in the space provided below. Take time to think about what you've read and restate it carefully before you write it. By writing key thoughts in your own words, you reinforce your learning. Review your outline before a quiz or examination.

Several important thoughts taken from the Chapter Objective 1 section are provided as an example to get you started. If there aren't enough dots (bullets), add more.

I. Define marketing, explain its origins and contemporary meanings.

. Marketing is more than just selling; it means working hard to satisfy consumer needs and wants, and to achieve your goals.

. Marketing is defined by the American Marketing Association as "...the process of planning and executing the conception, pricing, promotion and distribution of ideas, goods and services to create exchanges that satisfy individual and organizational objectives."

.

.

.

II. Identify the key foundation concepts of marketing.

.

.

.

.

III. Explain why it is important to study marketing.

IV. Discuss why and how marketing is still evolving.

V. Describe how marketers use the marketing mix variables to satisfy consumers and achieve organizational goals.

KEY TERMS

After studying Chapter 1, you should be able to define each of the following key terms and use them in describing marketing activities. In the space beside each key term, write your own definition of the term without referring to the textbook.

■ **KEY TERMS FOR YOU TO DEFINE**

Marketing

Consumer Insight

Value

Consumer Gap Analysis

Exchange

Products

Utility

Market

Marketplace

Demarketing

Need

Want

Marketing Mix Variables (Four Ps)

Production Period

Selling Period

Marketing Concept Period

Marketing Concept

Societal Marketing Concept

Target Market

Product

Price

Place

Promotion

CHAPTER QUESTIONS AND ACTIVITIES

This section provides you with a place to answer the questions posed in the textbook in the **Check Your Understanding** sections and in the **Discussion Questions, Mini-Cases,** and **What Do You Think?** at the end of the chapter. Space is also provided for your reactions to **Marketing Applications, Consumer Insights, International Marketing,** and **Marketing on the Internet.**

CHECK YOUR UNDERSTANDING

■ **Check Your Understanding 1.1**

1. In your own words, what is marketing?

2. Explain how sending a resume to a prospective employer is marketing. Who is the buyer? Who is the seller?

3. Does marketing occur when seven families on your street get together to have a garage sale? Explain.

■ **Check Your Understanding 1.2**

1. What are the foundation concepts of marketing?

2. Explain the concept of exchange.

3. Why is satisfaction such an important concept in marketing?

■ **Check Your Understanding 1.3**

1. Of the reasons given for studying marketing, identify the ones that are most important to you.

2. How can marketing contribute to a standard of living?

54

3. How is your daily life affected by marketing?

■ **Check Your Understanding 1.4**

1. Explain the focus and scope of the Individual and Organizational Eras of marketing.

2. What is the marketing concept? Give an example of a company that you believe is operating on this philosophy; explain your answer.

3. Should businesses adopt the societal marketing concept?

MARKETING APPLICATIONS

Even if your teacher does not assign the Marketing Applications in the textbook, you can learn about marketing by reading the **Applications**, thinking about the issues raised, summarizing the contents, and then answering one or more key questions about each **Application**. Learning by doing is one of the most effective ways to learn.

■ **MARKETING APPLICATION 1.1**

What is the issue raised by this **Marketing Application**?

What conclusions can you draw from this activity about obstacles to developing consumer insights?

■ MARKETING APPLICATION 1.2

What is the issue raised by this **Marketing Application**?

What conclusions can you draw from this activity about gaps in the marketplace?

■ MARKETING APPLICATION 1.3

What is the issue raised by this **Marketing Application**?

What conclusions can you draw from this activity about demarketing strategies?

■ MARKETING APPLICATION 1.4

What is the issue raised by this **Marketing Application**?

What conclusions can you draw from this activity about the value of customer satisfaction surveys in letting a company know how customers feel about their products?

■ MARKETING APPLICATION 1.5

What is the issue raised by this **Marketing Application**?

What conclusions can you draw from this activity about consumer letters as a way for a company to learn about consumer satisfaction with their products?

DISCUSSION QUESTIONS

1. What is being exchanged between each of the following pairs of sellers and buyers?
   a. Colleges - Students

   b. American Cancer Society - Contributors

   c. Presidential Candidate - Voters

   d. Mothers Against Drunk Driving (MADD) - General Driving Public

   e. Local Government Garbage Disposal Service - Citizens

2. "Marketing is responsible for our materialistic society." Comment on this statement.

3. Do each of the following perform marketing activities? If so, what is the goal of their marketing effort?
   a. Arthur Andersen (accounting firm)

   b. American Express (bank card)

    c.   Good Samaritan Hospital (not-for-profit public hospital)

    d.   U.S. Army

    e.   Toyota U.S.A. Motor Manufacturing Company

4. Is the societal marketing concept a realistic concept for a business to adopt? Why or why not?

5. Explain why consumer insights are important to marketing.

6. What types of utility are created by each of the following?
    a.   Blockbuster Video

    b.   Mr. Suds' automated, drive-through car wash

    c.   BancTwo Automatic Teller Machine.

7. Explain which is more difficult to market, an idea or a place.

8. Describe the foundation concepts of marketing.

9. If you were a marketing teacher, how would you explain to your class the importance of studying marketing?

10. Describe how marketing has evolved in the United States. Do you think it will continue to evolve?

MINI-CASES

■ **Mini-Case 1.1: 'Pig's Eye' Beats Out 'Landmark' As Customers' Favorite**

In your own words, summarize this case in the space below.

1. Is MBC using the marketing concept philosophy? Explain your answer.

2. Evaluate the mistakes made by MBC for each of the marketing mix variables (product, price, place, promotion).

3. How can MBC fix its mistakes? What changes should it make?

■ **Mini-Case 1.2: Twentysomethings: The Consumers That Marketers Almost Forgot**

In your own words, summarize this case in the space below.

1. Mazda ran a very conservative advertising campaign directed at baby boomers and used cues like a woman wearing pearls and classical music in the background. How might Mazda change their advertising for generation X targets?

2. How can marketers find out what the generation X market is really all about? What would it take to develop consumer insight about the twentysomethings?

WHAT DO YOU THINK?

In your own words, summarize the issue addressed in this WHAT DO YOU THINK?, then answer the questions.

. Is there a conflict between the marketing concept's focus on delivering customer satisfaction and the marketing of products that are potentially harmful to consumers?

. Whose marketing standards should be followed, those of the seller's country or the buyers?

. What do you think?

CONSUMER INSIGHTS, INTERNATIONAL MARKETING

■ CONSUMER INSIGHT 1.1

What is the issue raised by this **Consumer Insight**?

■ **CONSUMER INSIGHT 1.2**

What is the issue raised by this **Consumer Insight**?

■ **INTERNATIONAL MARKETING REPORT**

What is the issue raised by this **International Marketing Report**?

MARKETING ON THE INTERNET

What is the issue raised by this **Marketing On The Internet**?

CHAPTER 1
TEST YOURSELF

The Chapter 1 opening question is

What would your life be like if there were no marketing?

What is your answer to this question now that you have completed reading the chapter?

■ TRUE OR FALSE

For each of the following questions, print T (true) or F (false) on the line beside the number.

_____ 1. Marketing is one of the broadest areas of study in the business fields.

_____ 2. The open-air market was probably the starting point for the development of the term *market-ing*, which meant bringing your goods to market.

_____ 3. Marketing today refers only to activities of for-profit businesses.

_____ 4. Marketing activities create value.

_____ 5. For an exchange to occur, both buyer and seller must benefit from the transaction.

_____ 6. Typically, in the competitive U.S. marketplace, consumer demand exceeds product supply.

_____ 7. Consumer satisfaction is very important to marketers.

_____ 8. Marketing is only selling.

_____ 9. The marketing mix variables are the tactical tools that marketers use to achieve their strategic goals.

_____10. The marketing concept is an operating philosophy that puts customer satisfaction first.

■ COMPLETION

Complete each sentence by filling-in-the-blank.

11. Marketers try to identify _____ in the marketplace that represent consumers' unfilled needs and wants.

12. The worth added to products through marketing activities is called _____.

13. _____ is a voluntary trading of things of value between parties, with the expectation that the parties will be better off after the trade than before.

14. _____ are the things of value that the seller brings to a marketplace and the buyer needs or wants.

15. Product, price, place, and promotion are called the _____ _____ variables.

16. The _____ _____ is an operating philosophy that has customer satisfaction at its core.

17. The _____ _____ _____ has the goal of satisfying consumers <u>and</u> society.

64

18. Groups of consumers who are current or potential customers are also called a _____ market.

19. _____ is the marketing mix variable that refers to where, when, and how the product is made available to consumers.

20. _____ is the marketing mix variable that refers to how marketers communicate with consumers, and includes such activities as advertising, personal selling, sales promotions, and public relations.

■ MULTIPLE CHOICE

Circle the letter of the best answer.

21. Computers, television sets, shoes, and clothing are examples of products that are ____.
    a. services
    b. ideas
    c. goods
    d. experiences

22. Mayellen works the late shift at a local computer assembly plant. She does her grocery shopping at 2:00 AM, on her way home from work. Having the grocery open when she needs it represents ____ utility.
    a. place
    b. form
    c. possession
    d. time

23. A runner nearing the finish line of a 10K race feels the effects of the race and must have liquids to replace those lost during her exertions. This represents a ____, a desire or preference caused by a deprivation.
    a. need
    b. value
    c. want
    d. preference

24. According to Maslow's Hierarchy of Human Needs, advertisements that communicate messages about products that satisfy a consumer's need for success are appealing to
    a. biogenic/physiological needs.
    b. ego needs.
    c. social belonging needs.
    d. safety/security needs.

25. Job growth in marketing and sales is expected to grow 20.6 percent between 1992 and 2005. Factors contributing to the expected growth include
    a. huge increases in U.S. population.
    b. increased marketing by hospitals, schools, and governments.
    c. the end to all restrictions on immigration to the United States.
    d. reductions in foreign competition in the U.S. domestic market and abroad.

26. Marketing is a dynamic process that continues to evolve. The earliest period was mainly marketing by small businesses with a predominately local scope. This often is called the ___ era.
    a. organizational
    b. independent
    c. societal
    d. individual

27. From about the late 1870s through the late 1920s, the primary business operating philosophy was to increase output and efficiency in processes, products, and distribution. This is often called the ____ period.
    a. selling
    b. marketing
    c. production
    d. industrial

28. Marketing activities related to transporting and storing products are associated with the ____ function of marketing.
    a. exchange
    b. physical Distribution
    c. servicing
    d. production

29. Packaging, warranties and guarantees, and associated services are part of the ____ variable.
    a. product
    b. price
    c. place
    d. promotion

30. Marketing is traditionally directed toward stimulating consumer demand, not dampening it. However, when consumer demand exceeds product supply, marketers sometimes use ____ to reduce demand.
    a. contramarketing
    b. remarketing
    c. demarketing
    d. antimarketing

Note: Answers to the questions posed in this section appear in **PART III: Answers To Study Guide "Test Yourself" Questions** at the end of this *Study Guide.*

CHAPTER 2
MAKING MARKETING DECISIONS–DEVELOPING MARKETING PLANS

CHAPTER SUMMARY

Chapter 2 surveys characteristics of marketing decisions and plans. Decisions are choices between sets of alternatives. Marketing decisions and plans focus on the marketing functions of exchange, physical distribution, and servicing. Marketing decisions vary in their complexity, timing, focus, scope, risk, and participants. Plans are sets of decisions, blueprints for marketing actions. Plans and the planning process can help a business cope with uncertainty and prepare it to seize marketing opportunities. Marketers contribute to planning at all business levels. Marketing plans require performing a situation analysis, segmenting markets, selecting target markets, developing marketing mix strategies, writing a marketing plan, implementing the plan, and controlling the results. Marketing decisions and plans are influenced by what is happening in different environments. Internal environments are very close to the business and include its own operating areas as well as businesses in a multibusiness corporation. External environments include the immediate external environment, along with the greater domestic environment and international environment. The effects of these environments vary, along with the ability of a business to directly influence them. Environmental volatility is a potent factor that often works to undermine even the best laid plans.

CHAPTER OBJECTIVES

This chapter is organized around a series of numbered learning objectives. Each objective statement that follows includes space for you to restate the statement as a question, then answer it with a concise answer that also summarizes the text section.

Step 1   Restate the objective statement as a question.

Step 2   Read the corresponding section in the textbook.

Step 3   Based on what you have read, answer the objective question.

CHAPTER OBJECTIVES

1. Describe the characteristics of marketing decisions.

Question

Answer

2. Explain the importance of planning and describe the building blocks of plans.

Question

Answer

3. Describe how plans are developed.

Question

Answer

4. Discuss marketing planning at the business level.

Question

Answer

5. Distinguish between the different environments that affect marketing decisions and plans.

Question

Answer

■ **CHAPTER OUTLINE**

I. **Describe the characteristics of marketing decisions**

-
-
-
-
-

II. Explain the importance of planning horizons and describe the building blocks of plans

-

-

-

-

-

-

III. Explain how plans are developed

-

-

-

-

70

IV. Discuss marketing planning at the business level

-
  -
  -
  -
  -
  -

V. Distinguish between the different environments that affect marketing decisions and plans

-
  -
  -
  -

KEY TERMS

In the space beside each key term, write your own definition of the term <u>without referring to the textbook</u>.

■ **KEY TERMS FOR YOU TO DEFINE**

Decisions

Plans

Windows of Opportunity

Planning

Planning Horizons

Short-Range Plans

Annual Plans

Mid-Range Plans

Long-Range Plans

Goals

Objectives

Strategy

Tactics

Mission Statement

Distinctive Competencies

Situation Analysis

SWOT

Market Segmentation

Marketing Plan

Internal Marketing Environments

External Marketing Environments

Personal Use Consumers

Business and Organizational Consumers

CHAPTER QUESTIONS AND ACTIVITIES

This section provides you with a place to answer the questions posed in the textbook in the **Check Your Understanding** sections and in the **Discussion Questions, Mini-Cases,** and **What Do You Think?** at the end of the chapter. Space is also provided for your reactions to **Marketing Applications, Consumer Insights, International Marketing,** and **Marketing on the Internet.**

CHECK YOUR UNDERSTANDING

■ Check Your Understanding 2.1

1. Explain this statement: "Marketing decisions are as varied as the profession itself."

2. What is a window of opportunity? Why are windows of opportunity so important to marketers?

3. Explain why plans are called *blueprints.*

■ **Check Your Understanding 2.2**

1. Why is planning important to achieving marketing success?

2. Should all organizations plan ahead? Explain your answer.

3. What differences are there among short-range, mid-range, and long-range planning horizons?

■ **Check Your Understanding 2.3**

1. How are goals and objectives related?

2. What is the difference between strategy and tactics?

3. Give examples of how individuals also use strategies and tactics, and goals and objectives in their daily lives.

1. What is a mission statement? How does a mission statement affect marketing activities?

2. Peter Drucker believes that a business should be defined by answering three questions. What are these questions?

3. Do nonprofit organizations and governments have mission statements? Should they? Explain your answer.

MARKETING APPLICATIONS

■ MARKETING APPLICATION 2.1

What is the issue raised by this **Marketing Application**?

What conclusions can you draw from this activity about some retailers' efforts to satisfy consumers?

■ MARKETING APPLICATION 2.2

What is the issue raised by this **Marketing Application**?

What conclusions can you draw from this activity about planning? Is it an important activity? Should all businesses plan?

■ MARKETING APPLICATION 2.3

What is the issue raised by this **Marketing Application**?

What conclusions can you draw from this activity about the challenge of writing a useful, effective mission statement?

■ MARKETING APPLICATION 2.4

What is the issue raised by this **Marketing Application**?

What conclusions can you draw from this activity about environmental factors? Can they upset even the best planning efforts by a business or organization?

DISCUSSION QUESTIONS

1. Marketers make many different kinds of decisions. Describe some of them.

2. Why is it important to do the right thing rather than just do things right?

3. Why do some individuals plan for their personal lives? Why do marketers plan?

4. Why is a mission statement important to a business?

5. What is a distinctive competency? List a distinctive competency of each of the following

a. Dallas Cowboys Football Team

b. The University of California

c. The U.S. Army

d. Ben and Jerry's Ice Cream Company

6. What is environmental analysis? Why is it so important?

7. What is the most important outcome for marketing decisions? Why?

8. Why is it important for marketers to carefully identify their target markets?

9. Describe the major parts of a marketing plan. How are these parts related?

10. List some external environmental factors that influence the marketing decisions of each of the following
   a. McDonald's

   b. A local bank

   c. A local police force

MINI-CASES

■ **Mini-Case 2.1: Small Can Be Beautiful for Niche Marketers**

In your own words, summarize this case in the space below.

1. What do you think is in LLB's mission statement?

2. What environmental factors might influence LLB's business?

3. Do you think that small niche businesses plan? Do they have marketing plans? Explain your answers.

■ **Mini-Case 2.2: Euro Disney: Even a Master Marketer's Plans Can Go Wrong**

In your own words, summarize this case in the space below.

1. Disney's Older parks (in Orlando, Anaheim, and Tokyo) are all profitable. What effect might their profitability have had on Disney's decisions for Euro Disney?

2. Even a company of Disney's size cannot directly affect the European economy. Does this mean that what a marketer can't control shouldn't be considered in planning?

WHAT DO YOU THINK?

In your own words, summarize the issue addressed in this WHAT DO YOU THINK?, then answer the questions.

. What do you think about the practice of product autopsy? Is it a good idea? Why or why not?

CONSUMER INSIGHTS, INTERNATIONAL MARKETING

■ CONSUMER INSIGHT 2.1

What is the issue raised by this **Consumer Insight**?

■ CONSUMER INSIGHT 2.2

What is the issue raised by this **Consumer Insight**?

What is the issue raised by this **International Marketing Report**?

MARKETING ON THE INTERNET

What is the issue raised by this **Marketing On The Internet**?

CHAPTER 2
TEST YOURSELF

The Chapter 2 opening question is

Why is making the right marketing decision sometimes so difficult to do?

What is your answer to this question now that you have completed reading the chapter?

■ TRUE OR FALSE

For each of the following questions, print T (true) or F (false) on the line beside the number.

_____ 1. Businesses that fail to adapt are usually discarded by a marketplace that has little tolerance for complacency.

_____ 2. Marketing decisions involve activities in the three broad marketing functions of exchange, physical distribution, and promotion.

_____ 3. Strategic planning still has not been widely accepted by most of the Fortune 1000 companies.

_____ 4. As planning horizons increase, there is greater certainty about what may actually happen in the period covered.

_____ 5. Marketing planning occurs at all levels in a corporation, at the top corporate level, business level, and operations level.

_____ 6. Goals and objectives are ends that are being sought.

_____ 7. Consumer insights can provide valuable information in the formulation of a mission statement.

_____ 8. Market segments must be formed before a target market can be selected.

_____ 9. PRIZM is a targeting tool that identifies consumer segments by matching consumer characteristics to zip codes demographics across the country.

_____10. The executive summary in a marketing plan is a one or two page summary of the key points in the plan.

■ COMPLETION

Complete each sentence by filling-in-the-blank.

11. Bounded, short-range, specific goals are called _____.

12. A _____ _____ is a written definition of the present state of a business and indicates what the company should look like in the future.

13. The largest and most efficient collector of information in the world, the U.S. _____, also has established a high profile position on the Internet as an information provider.

14. A _____ analysis is a systematic analysis that requires evaluating the environments (internal and external) within which the business operates and identifying strengths, weaknesses, threats, and opportunities.

15. The process of grouping consumers by shared characteristics is _____ _____.

16. A _____ _____ is a blueprint for using the marketing mix variables to satisfy consumers and achieve organizational goals.

17. Channel members, suppliers, customers, and competitors are part of a business's _____ _____ environment.

18. Foreign competitors and suppliers are part of a business's external _____ environment.

19. People making purchases on behalf of their companies, to use in production, operations, or for resale are called _____ _____ consumers.

20. People purchasing products for their own or family use, or to give as gifts to others are called _____ _____ consumers.

■ MULTIPLE CHOICE

Circle the letter of the best answer.

21. Which of the following occupations is NOT associated with the exchange marketing function?
    a. Advertising account manager.
    b. Brand manager.
    c. Freight forwarder.
    d. Retail buyer.

22. Mid-range plans are usually made for _____ years in the future.
    a. Five to ten.
    b. One to two.
    c. Two to five.
    d. Twenty-five or more.

23. Which of the following is NOT part of promotion planning?
    a. Advertising plans.
    b. Personal selling plans.
    c. Direct marketing plans.
    d. Product price plans.

24. _____ are long-range, generally unbounded ends to be achieved. They are priorities for future actions.
    a. Objectives.
    b. Goals.
    c. Strategy.
    d. Tactics.

25. Which of the following is NOT a step typically associated with developing companywide plans?
    a. Develop a mission statement.
    b. Establish priorities - actionable goals and objectives.
    c. Develop a strategic plan.
    d. Perform competitive espionage.

26. Do Right Pest Control is a market leader in pest control, well known as an innovator in using natural, organic methods for controlling house and garden insect pests. Do Right uses television advertising to tell consumers what it does best. It is informing consumers about its _____ _____.
    a. Distinctive competencies.
    b. Competitive disadvantages.
    c. Distracting capabilities.
    d. Competitive difficulties.

27. A SWOT analysis is a systematic situation analysis that evaluates a business's ____, ____, ____, and ____.
   a. strengths, weaknesses, opportunities, threats
   b. successes, weaknesses, opportunities, threats
   c. strengths, weaknesses, opportunities, timing
   d. strengths, weaknesses, organization, threats

28. Which of the following statements about marketing plans is FALSE? A marketing plan
   a. is a blueprint for how the marketing mix variables will be used to satisfy consumers.
   b. specifies strategies, marketing actions, and product matches.
   c. is the long-range component of a business's strategic plan and is written for periods of 5 to 10 years, or longer.
   d. it is only a blueprint for action and not a substitute for leadership.

29. The three interrelated processes of marketing planning, implementation, and ____ are essential marketing management activities.
   a. control
   b. exchange
   c. promotion
   d. segmentation

30. The economy, science/technology, culture/society, the public, and the government, politics, and laws are all part of a business's
   a. immediate internal environment
   b. immediate external environment
   c. greater domestic environment
   d. international environment

Note: Answers to the questions posed in this section appear in **PART III: Answers to Study Guide "Test Yourself" Questions** at the end of this *Study Guide*.

CHAPTER 3
SEGMENTING THE MARKET: CONSUMER BUYING DECISIONS

CHAPTER SUMMARY

In this chapter you will learn about consumers who are the targets of marketing activities. Consumers are often grouped into two broad segments: business and organization consumers, a market that includes industrial, reseller, government, and not-for-profit markets; and personal use consumers, over 260 million people in the United States alone. Many marketers direct their offers toward a mass market, most group consumers into segments, then target those segments with the greatest purchase potential. Segments are formed by grouping consumers who share demographic, psychographic, geographic, behavioral, or a combination of characteristics. Marketers try to influence consumers' perceptions of their products so the products will be favorably positioned compared to the competition. Consumer satisfaction is a primary goal of marketing activities in both types of consumer markets. Not all consumer behavior is rational or acceptable. Deviant consumer behaviors represent actions that are different from acceptable norms and may also represent illegal behaviors.

Both business/organization and personal use consumers must decide whether to make, lease, or buy products. Some product purchases are rebuys, others are modified rebuys, or new task buys. Some purchase decisions are made independently while others involve people working together in formal or informal buying centers. Steps in the purchase decision process vary. Most personal use consumer purchase decisions are far less formal than those made by business/organization consumers, while the latter often face greater risk and uncertainty in making a purchase decision.

Some influences on business/organization purchase decisions are organizational, particularly the priorities and strategies established for the buying unit, organizational characteristics, and demand. While most business/organization purchase decisions are rational and objective, human emotions can affect the outcomes. Professional buyers are evaluated by the effectiveness of their purchase decisions about the core product and associated services such as terms of delivery, installations, and product guarantees.

Consumer behavior is all the activities involved in selecting, purchasing, evaluating, and disposing of products. Personal use consumers experience many different external influences on their behavior and purchase decisions. External influences may affect many consumers concurrently and often, similarly. Important social influences are the family, reference groups, and social class. Culture and microculture also affect consumer behaviors. Other external influences are those applied by marketers, the buying situation, technology, product supply, and even the weather.

Internal influences are personal, unique, and not observable. These are psychological factors that sometimes can be inferred by observing consumer behavior and include needs and wants, involvement, perception, learning, attitudes and attitude change, and personality. Marketers must understand the nature of these influences in order to be able to understand consumers so they can try to satisfy them.

CHAPTER OBJECTIVES

This chapter is organized around a series of numbered learning objectives. Each objective is stated, with blank space provided for you to restate the statement as a question, then answer it with a concise answer that also summarizes the text section.

Step 1: Restate the objective statement as a question.

Step 2: Read the corresponding section in the textbook.

Step 3: Based on what you have read, answer the objective question.

1. Describe the two segments of consumers: business/organization and personal use.

Question

Answer

2. Identify the characteristics of consumer purchase decisions.

Question

Answer

3. Describe influences on business/organization consumers.

Question

Answer

4. Recognize external influences on personal use consumers.

Question

Answer

5. Recognize internal influences on personal use consumers.

Question

Answer

CHAPTER OUTLINE

I. Describe the two segments of consumers: business/organization and personal use.

•

•

•

II. Identify the characteristics of consumer purchase decisions.

-

-

-

-

-

-

III. Describe influences on business/organization consumers.

-

-

IV. **Recognize external influences on personal use consumers.**

V. **Recognize internal influences on personal use consumers.**

KEY TERMS

In the space beside each key term, write your own definition of the term <u>without referring to the textbook</u>.

KEY TERMS FOR YOU TO DEFINE

Target Marketing

Business

Organization

Positioning

Consumer Satisfaction

Cognitive Dissonance

Deviant Consumer Behavior

Straight Rebuys

New Task Buys

Modified Rebuys

Buying Center

Derived Demand

Elastic Demand

Inelastic Demand

Fluctuating Demand

Impulse Purchase

Consumer Behavior

Demographics

Baby Boomers

CHAPTER QUESTIONS AND ACTIVITIES

This section provides you with a place to answer the questions posed in the textbook in the **Check Your Understanding** sections and in the **Discussion Questions, Mini-Cases,** and **What Do You Think?** at the end of the chapter. Space is also provided for your reactions to **Marketing Applications, Consumer Insights, International Marketing,** and **Marketing on the Internet.**

CHECK YOUR UNDERSTANDING

■ **Check Your Understanding 3.1**

1. Why do some marketers prefer to mass market their products?

2. How are business/organization consumers classified?

3. Explain why consumer satisfaction is so important to marketers.

■ **Check Your Understanding 3.2**

1. Describe these alternatives: make, lease, or buy.

2. Contrast rebuy and new task buying decisions.

3. What is a buying center?

■ **Check Your Understanding 3.3**

1. How can a mission statement direct purchase decisions?

2. Explain the terms: derived, elastic, and inelastic demand.

3. Describe other purchase factors that influence business/organization consumers.

■ **Check Your Understanding 3.4**

1. Describe the types of external influences on personal use consumer purchase decisions.

2. How can life stages influence a family's purchases?

3. Explain how roles, reference groups, and opinion leaders influence personal use consumers.

■ **Check Your Understanding 3.5**

1. What are needs? How are they related to motives?

2. How does involvement influence perception?

3. What is an attitude? Can consumer attitudes be changed?

MARKETING APPLICATIONS

■ MARKETING APPLICATION 3.1

What is the issue raised by this **Marketing Application**?

What conclusions can you draw from this activity about the similarities between the two broad groups of consumers when they make routine purchases?

■ MARKETING APPLICATION 3.2

What is the issue raised by this **Marketing Application**?

What conclusions can you draw from this activity about the effectiveness of fear advertisements in influencing consumer purchase decisions?

■ MARAKETING APPLICATION 3.3

What is the issue raised by this **Marketing Application**?

What conclusions can you draw from this activity about the influence of the roles people play on their purchase decisions? Could the commonality of role types be a useful basis for targeting consumers?

■ MARKETING APPLICATION 3.4

What is the issue raised by this **Marketing Application**?

What conclusions can you draw from this activity about the impact of multicultural diversity on consumer behavior?

■ MARKETING APPLICATION 3.5

What is the issue raised by this **Marketing Application**?

What conclusions can you draw from this activity about information overload and the effect of too much information on consumer decision making?

DISCUSSION QUESTIONS

1. Explain why you think consumer behavior is such a puzzle to many marketers.

2. Can someone be both a business/organization and personal use consumer? Explain your answer.

3. What is deviant consumer behavior? Why is it important that marketers be aware of such behaviors?

4. Explain the difference between a make, lease, or buy decision by both consumer segments.

5. Pretend that your school is purchasing its first-ever schoolwide computer system. This system will be used for academic, administrative, research, and teaching purposes. Who should sit on the school's buying center committee?

6. Of the following product purchases, which has the highest financial risk, the highest physical risk, or the highest social risk?
   a. New clothes to wear on a first date

   b. New 486SX personal computer

   c. Fifteen-year old used car

7. Jim is walking through Cherry Blossom Mall. A pair of boots in a store window attract his eye. He doesn't need boots, but decides to try them on. He likes them so much, he purchases them. Is this an impulse purchase? Explain your answer?

8. What is the baby boom generation? Why is it of such interest to marketers?

9. Who influenced your choice to attend school? What were your internal influences? Your external influences?

10. What is a multigenerational family? What different opinions might members of such a family give when faced with a decision about a family vacation?

MINI-CASES

■ **Mini-Case 3.1: What Has Happened to the Fat-Conscious Consumer?**

In your own words, summarize this case in the space below.

1. What do you think is happening to consumers' commitment to eating healthy?

2. If you were a marketer of a line of healthy foods, would you abandon the healthy food market?

3. Do you think this trend toward more flavorful foods will last? Why or why not? Can you explain your answer in terms of demographics?

■ **Mini-Case 3.2: Gender Differences Show Up in Consumer Behaviors**

In your own words, summarize this case in the space below.

1. Do you think social pressures could have anything to do with these gender differences?

2. Are these gender differences important to marketers? Explain your answer.

3. Will some of these differences change as more men have to do the grocery shopping and more women have to use computers?

WHAT DO YOU THINK?

In your own words, summarize the issue addressed in this WHAT DO YOU THINK?, then answer the questions.

. Why do you think consumers say one thing but won't follow through with a purchase?

. How would you define a target market for EcoSport's clothes? What characteristics define their customers?

. What related products might be sold along with the clothes?

. Is this a good business to be in now? **WHAT DO YOU THINK?**

■ **CONSUMER INSIGHT 3.1**

What is the issue raised by this **Consumer Insight**?

■ **CONSUMER INSIGHT 3.2**

What is the issue raised by this **Consumer Insight**?

■ INTERNATIONAL MARKETING REPORT

What is the issue raised by this **International Marketing Report**?

MARKETING ON THE INTERNET

What is the issue raised by this **Marketing On The Internet**?

CHAPTER 3

TEST YOURSELF

The Chapter 3 opening question is

Why is it that despite all our knowledge about consumers, they still are often a puzzle to marketers?

What is your answer to this question now that you have completed reading the chapter?

■ TRUE OR FALSE

For each of the following questions, print T (true) or F (false) on the line beside the number.

_____ 1. Fluctuating demand reflects general economic conditions in which demand usually rises when the economy is robust and falls when the economy is weak.

_____ 2. Although a business/organization consumer may make an impulse purchase, personal use consumers rarely make impulse purchases.

_____ 3. For the business/organization consumer, product quality often means how well a product conforms to technical specifications, sometimes with a zero tolerance for defects.

_____ 4. Social classes in the United States are very rigid, which means that once consumers are categorized within a social class, they can be targeted as a member of that class for a lifetime.

_____ 5. Culture and microculture have no effect on personal use consumers' purchase decisions.

_____ 6. Needs are gaps between reality and a desired state that create a tension the individual seeks to release through goal-directed behavior.

_____ 7. Typically, consumers are very selective in their perceptions, which means that consumers exposed to the same advertisement may have very different responses to it depending on how they perceive the advertisement.

_____ 8. Almost all consumer behavior is learned.

_____ 9. Marketers can change consumers' attitudes only if the attitude is very closely tied to the consumer's self-concept or the consumer is highly involved with the attitude object.

_____10. Personality has been found to be a very good predictor of what consumers buy and why.

■ COMPLETION

Complete each sentence by filling-in-the-blank.

11. Repeat purchases of products that are bought and consumed on a regular basis without a change in the order are called _____ rebuys or _____ orders.

12. In the family buying process, different family members may play different roles. For example, someone plays the role of the _____ who collects and distributes information about the product and purchase.

13. _____ demand occurs when demand for one product increases demand for other products.

14. _____ demand exists for products that consumers consider essential, meaning that they have a higher tolerance for price changes, so when prices rise, consumers still purchase because the products are essential.

15. _____ _____ is all of the activities involved in selecting, purchasing, evaluating, and disposing of products.

16. Secondary social groups such as work groups, religious groups, and clubs that influence consumers are also called _____ groups.

17. Socially influenced needs are called _____.

18. Consumers select, organize, interpret information, and give meaning to it through the process called _____.

19. Any change in behavior that results from experience or the interpretation of experience is called _____.

20. _____ is a learned predisposition to respond to stimuli and behave in a certain way.

■ MULTIPLE CHOICE

Circle the letter of the best answer.

21. Business/organization consumers are classified into major groups. Which of the following is NOT a major group in the business or organization consumer market?
    a. The government market.
    b. The reseller market.
    c. The household market.
    d. The industrial market.

22. Dejuan is head of marketing for Baring's Microbrewery and Fine Beers. He is in the process of selecting which well-defined groups of potential customers will be sent promotional information about the company's products. Dejuan is ____ the company's most promising markets.
    a. targeting
    b. segmenting
    c. implementing
    d. controlling

23. AdWorks Advertising is preparing a print advertising campaign directed at a group of consumers described solely by their shared *demographic* characteristics. *Demographic* characteristics usually include such consumer information as
    a. their gender, age, and income.
    b. in what region of the country they live.
    c. their lifestyle.
    d. their brand loyalty and purchase behaviors.

24. Charlie has just made his first new car purchase. He is having second thoughts about spending so much for an automobile. This is a very costly automobile and he will be in debt for the next three years. Maybe he should have bought a good secondhand car. Charlie is experiencing
    a. consumer satisfaction.
    b. cognitive acceptance.
    c. consumer perception.
    d. cognitive dissonance.

25. All of the following are considered deviant behaviors. Which is NOT specifically a retailer-directed deviant consumer behavior?
    a. Writing bad checks.
    b. Compulsive shopping.
    c. Switching price tags.
    d. Not reporting favorable billing errors.

26. Moreland Pearls is well known for producing fine jewelry from pearls, gold, and silver. The company is expanding its jewelry lines and will begin making jewelry from semi-precious minerals such as black onyx, hematite, and garnet. In order to start this new operation, they must purchase a high priced mineral tumbler. This means collecting information and considering alternatives before making the purchase. This purchase is an example of a
    a. straight rebuy
    b. modified new buy
    c. modified rebuy
    d. new task buy

27. Marta is a member of the buying center at Moreland Pearls who will be making the decision about purchasing the new mineral tumbler. She knows more about this product than anyone else in the company, so the other members of the buying center are listening very carefully to her comments. She is playing the buying center role of
    a. initiator
    b. gatekeeper
    c. influencer
    d. user

28. Patsy is taking her winter clothes out of storage and airing them to get rid of the mothball smell. She has lost weight since last winter and intends to keep it off! She tries on her winter coat, only to find that it is far too big for her. At what step is Patsy in the consumer purchase decision model?
    a. Problem recognition.
    b. Information search.
    c. Identification of alternatives.
    d. Behavioral intention.

29. Joe and Delinda are celebrating their 20th anniversary by moving into a larger house so that each of their three teenage children can have their own bedroom. Joe and Delinda are in the _____ lifestage.
    a. empty nest
    b. full nest
    c. young marrieds
    d. young singles

30. There are many different types of external influences on consumer behavior. Which of the following is a *situational influence* on a consumer's behavior?
    a. A new and highly effective advertising campaign.
    b. The opinions of close friends.
    c. The consumer's membership in the middle class.
    d. A thunderstorm that knocks out the electricity to cash registers and closes the store.

Note: Answers to the questions posed in this section appear in **PART III: Answers to Study Guide "Test Yourself" Questions** at the end of this *Study Guide*.

THE MARKETING ENVIRONMENT

CHAPTER SUMMARY

Marketing is important to society because it helps deliver the standard of living that most Americans enjoy. Micromarketing is the way marketing connects a business, its suppliers, distributors, and consumers in activities designed to deliver consumer satisfaction. Macromarketing is marketing on a broader, societal level that describes how marketing contributes to the economy and societal welfare by balancing supply and demand.

Marketers are granted broad rights in society, but they are also expected to act legally, ethically, and responsibly. Some businesses take this societal obligation very seriously and make it an integral part of their business and marketing activities. Most marketers behave ethically, adhering to the unwritten principles and values that govern and bring order to society. Marketers abide by a written professional code of conduct as well as codes of behavior established within their business or organization. Self-regulation, an important behavioral monitor, is also practiced by such groups as local Better Business Bureaus and trade associations.

Government controls marketing activities through laws, rules, and regulations. Formal legal controls cannot possibly encompass every activity that occurs in a complex marketplace, such as the United States. As a result, situations occur for which no clear behavioral guidelines exit. This can lead to ethical dilemmas for marketers and sometimes, ethical lapses. Laws are formal statements that guide actions and set limits and penalties for infractions. Federal business laws are procompetitive and many are designed to protect consumers. The Federal Trade Commission is the federal regulatory body that most directly controls marketing, and includes competitive and consumer protection activities. State and local laws, rules, and regulations control marketing activities within these jurisdictions. Regulations are the rules, standards, and guidelines that government agencies issue to implement laws.

Consumers sometimes suffer serious consequences from the imbalance in the marketplace caused by the advantages sellers have over buyers. Consumerism, a response to consumer abuses in the marketplace, is embodied in the cooperation of concerned individuals and organizations with many diverse interests who respond to issues of shared distress. President John Kennedy was the first incumbent president to send a formal message to the Congress identifying rights that consumers should be free to enjoy.

There are many contemporary societal issues involving marketing that capture the public imagination at various times. Three issues of lasting concern are green marketing, the marketing of harmful products, and marketing to children.

CHAPTER OBJECTIVES

This chapter is organized around a series of numbered learning objectives. Each objective statement that follows includes space for you to restate the statement as a question, then answer it with a concise answer that also summarizes the text section.

Step 1: Restate the objective statement as a question.

Step 2: Read the corresponding section in the textbook.

Step 3: Based on what you have read, answer the objective question.

1. **Define the dual roles of marketing in society: micromarketing and macromarketing.**

   Question

   Answer

2. **Describe the rights, responsibilities, and ethical dilemmas of marketers.**

   Question

   Answer

3. **Identify government controls on marketing.**

   Question

   Answer

4. Explain consumerism and the Consumer Bill of Rights.

Question

Answer

5. Identify some important contemporary societal issues involving marketing.

Question

Answer

CHAPTER OUTLINE

I. Marketing plays roles at the micro and macro levels of society.

-
-
-
-
-
-

II. Describe the rights, responsibilities, and ethical dilemmas of marketers.

-
-
-

III. Identify governmental controls on marketing.

IV. Explain consumerism and the Consumer Bill of Rights.

113

V. Identify some important contemporary societal issues involving marketing.

114

KEY TERMS

In the space beside each key term, write your own definition of the term <u>without referring to the textbook</u>.

■ **KEY TERMS FOR YOU TO DEFINE**

Society

Ethical Dilemmas

Micromarketing

Macromarketing

Materialism

Ethics

Laws

Regulations

Consumerism

Consumer Bill of Rights

Green Marketing

CHAPTER QUESTIONS AND ACTIVITIES

This section provides you with a place to answer the questions posed in the textbook in the **Check Your Understanding** sections and in the **Discussion Questions, Mini-Cases,** and **What Do You Think?** at the end of the chapter. Space is also provided for your reactions to **Marketing Applications, Consumer Insights, International Marketing,** and **Marketing on the Internet.**

CHECK YOUR UNDERSTANDING

■ **Check Your Understanding 4.1**

1. Distinguish between the dual societal roles of marketing: micro and macro.

2. Should marketers be concerned when consumers believe that marketing is not working well for them? Explain your answer.

3. How does society benefit from marketing activities?

■ **Check Your Understanding 4.2**

1. What rights do marketers have in the United States?

2. Discuss marketing's societal responsibilities.

3. What kinds of ethical dilemmas do marketers sometimes face?

■ **Check Your Understanding 4.3**

1. Compare and contrast laws and regulations.

2. Identify some federal laws that affect marketing.

3. What federal agency exerts the greatest control over marketing?

■ **Check Your Understanding 4.4**

1. Define consumerism.

2. Describe the major consumerism periods in U.S. history.

3. Identify the rights specified in the Consumer Bill of Rights.

■ **Check Your Understanding 4.5**

    1. What is green marketing?

    2. Should all products that *could* be harmful to consumers be banned?

    3. Should marketers be allowed to target children?

MARKETING APPLICATIONS

■ **MARKETING APPLICATION 4.1**

What is the issue raised by this **Marketing Application**?

What conclusions can you draw from this activity about problems in the marketplace? What are the most common problems and how serious are they?

■ MARKETING APPLICATION 4.2

What is the issue raised by this **Marketing Application**?

What conclusions can you draw from this activity about the societal contributions made by businesses generally and in particular, in your community?

■ MARKETING APPLICATION 4.3

What is the issue raised by this Marketing Application?

What conclusions can you draw from this activity about professional codes of ethics? How effective do you think they are in regulating the behaviors of their members?

■ MARKETING APPLICATION 4.4

What is the issue raised by this Marketing Application?

What conclusions can you draw from this activity about the work of Better Business Bureaus in helping consumers resolve problems they experience in the marketplace?

■ MARKETING APPLICATION 4.5

What is the issue raised by this **Marketing Application**?

What conclusions can you draw from this activity about how businesses identify the laws and regulations that govern their activities?

DISCUSSION QUESTIONS

1. Why is the buyer (consumer) often at a disadvantage in an exchange with a seller?

2. Identify some of the criticisms leveled at marketing, and discuss how they might be corrected.

3. Should consumers be satisfied all the time? Should the marketer work to accomplish this goal? Explain your answers.

4. What is materialism? Is it good or bad?

5. What are some types of controls on marketing?

6. Explain how some things that are unethical might still be legal?

7. Are all marketers evil? If not, what explanations could be offered for the mistakes they make?

8. Is price skimming illegal? Is it ethical? Is it good marketing?

9. Discuss how marketers are often caught in crossfires. Explain how this can affect their ability to make the right decisions.

10. Compare and contrast the societal marketing concept and the marketing concept. Do you think that the societal marketing concept will be readily accepted by all businesses? Why or why not?

MINI-CASES

■ **Mini-Case 4.1: Diet Disasters: The FTC, FDA, and Others Take Action**

In your own words, summarize this case in the space below.

1. Why is there such an obsession with thinness in the United States?

2. Is diet marketing legal? Is it ethical?

3. Do you think the antidiet movement in the United States will grow? Explain your answer.

■ **Mini-Case 4.2: Fear Appeals Sell Products**

In your own words, summarize this case in the space below.

1. Do consumers react to fear appeals in the same way?

2. Are fear appeals legal? Are they ethical?

3. Do fear appeals exploit consumers' weaknesses, or do they instead use powerful images to market important products?

WHAT DO YOU THINK?

*In your own words, summarize the issue addressed in this **WHAT DO YOU THINK?**, then answer the questions.*

. Should consumer product testing magazines accept products from manufacturers for testing?

. Should consumer product testing magazines accept advertisements from manufacturers whose products they test?

CONSUMER INSIGHTS, INTERNATIONAL MARKETING

■ **CONSUMER INSIGHT 4.1**

What is the issue raised by this Consumer Insight?

■ **INTERNATIONAL MARKETING REPORT**

What is the issue raised by this **International Marketing Report?**

MARKETING ON THE INTERNET

What is the issue raised by this **Marketing On The Internet?**

CHAPTER 4
TEST YOURSELF

The Chapter 4 opening questions are

What is the role of marketing in society?
Does marketing benefit or blemish society?

What are your answers to these questions now that you have completed reading the chapter?

■ TRUE OR FALSE

For each of the following questions, print T (true) or F (false) on the line beside the number.

_____ 1. Marketing activities are easily criticized because they are more visible to consumers than most other business areas and because they deal with sensitive issues like pricing, advertising, and selling.

_____ 2. Macromarketing is the way marketing connects a business, its suppliers, distributors, and consumers in activities designed to deliver satisfaction, as seen from the perspective of the individual marketer, consumer groups, the business or organization, and the channel of distribution.

_____ 3. In an ideal world, buyers and sellers should be on a fair and equal footing in the marketplace; however, in reality the seller often is at a disadvantage.

_____ 4. It is not necessary to address criticisms of marketing because there are so many consumers in the U.S. marketplace that a few consumer complaints will not hurt profits.

_____ 5. Generally, marketers may compete in any way as long as they do not break any laws, do adhere to existing rules and regulations, and don't harm consumers, society, or the competitive environment.

_____ 6. Although social programs undertaken by businesses can be costly, they can also be beneficial marketing tools.

_____ 7. Ethics often are situation specific, which sometimes makes it difficult to clearly determine the right and wrong of a situation.

_____ 8. International marketers are lucky because when they enter foreign markets, they do not face ethical dilemmas because foreign laws and regulations are very clear and govern all possible situations.

_____ 9. A code of ethics for marketing represents a subset of all the codes that influence marketers.

_____10. Marketers are bound by federal laws that have nationwide jurisdiction, state and local laws that have jurisdiction in the states in which the business operates.

■ COMPLETION

Complete each sentence by filling-in-the-blank.

11. A _____ is a political, geographical, and social entity defined by the rules, regulations, values, and behaviors its people accept and live by.

12. Marketers often face _____ _____, difficult situations in which there are valid but conflicting alternatives and it may not be clear which action or decision is right.

13. A preference for material possessions over spiritual and intellectual pursuits is called _____.

14. _____ are the usually unwritten rules of conduct that a society enforces to maintain order.

15. _____ are formal statements that guide actions and set limits and penalties for infractions.

16. Procompetitive laws began with the _____ Antitrust Act of 1890.

17. More than any other federal agency, the _____ is most directly involved in marketing activities.

18. Former Senator Charles H. Perch is credited with defining _____ as "a broad reaction against bureaucratic neglect and corporate disregard of the rights of the public."

19. President _____ was the first sitting president to send a formal message about consumer rights to the U.S. Congress.

20. _____ marketing is the term used to describe the activities of marketers who offer products that are environmentally friendly rather than environmentally harmful.

■ MULTIPLE CHOICE

Circle the letter of the best answer.

21. Patrice is an economist with a large Washington, D.C. research organization. It is his task to study how marketing contributes to our economic system and overall societal welfare. Patrice is studying _____.
    a. micromarketing
    b. demarketing
    c. remarketing
    d. macromarketing

22. Figure 4.1 (page 107 of the text) identifies ethical issues in marketing as cited in a recent survey. The top ethical issue, the one causing marketers the most difficulty, is _____.
    a. advertising
    b. bribery
    c. fairness
    d. honesty

23. Which of the following does NOT illustrate a type of complaint involving the marketing mix variables?
    a. Sellers are not on an equal footing with buyers in the marketplace.
    b. Products are unsafe, copycat, of poor quality, or environmentally unsafe.
    c. Place restrictions limit where products are offered.
    d. Promotion is overly aggressive.

24. Which of the following is NOT a right granted marketers in a competitive, free market system?
    a. The right to offer product guarantees and services postsale as desired, or not.
    b. The right to price products as desired, as long as the price doesn't harm competition or consumers.
    c. The right to promote products as desired in any medium as long as needed, provided there is no deception or fraud.
    d. The right to engage in any practice in the short run, even if it harms consumers and is anticompetitive, as long as the marketer is proconsumer and procompetitive in the long run.

25. A recent survey shows that about _____ percent of the business respondents believe that 'good' companies have an obligation to 'give back' to society.
    a. 76
    b. 50
    c. 24
    d. 97

26. Which of the following businesses donates all profits, after-taxes, from product sales to educational and charitable purposes?
    a. Ben & Jerry's.
    b. Celestial Seasonings.
    c. Newman's Own.
    d. Coca-Cola.

27. What is the best advice for U.S. marketers doing business in any foreign country, when they are approached by someone who wants a payoff (bribe) for doing business with them. "If you are approached for a bribe, _____.
    a. "Don't think about it."
    b. "Give it, but don't tell anyone."
    c. "Give it, but tell only your boss."
    d. "Don't give it, but tell the person trying to collect a bribe that you expect money to keep quiet about the attempt."

28. Which of the following is the first rule of professional ethics as stated in "Responsibilities of the Marketer" in the American Marketing Association's Code of Ethics? Marketers' professional conduct must be guided by
    a. Avoidance of false and misleading advertising.
    b. Treating outside clients and suppliers fairly.
    c. The basic rule of professional ethics: not knowingly to do harm.
    d. Not using coercion in the marketing channel.

29. Which of the following statements is NOT correct?
    a. The Lanham Act gives trademark protection to businesses while protecting consumers from unknowingly purchasing fraudulently branded products.
    b. The Federal Trade Commission Act deregulates natural gas, airlines, motor carriers, railroads, and banks.
    c. The Nutritional Labeling and Education Act requires nutritional labels on foods and prohibits exaggerated health claims.
    d. The Consumer Product Safety Commission Act established the Consumer Product Safety Commission which regulates product safety.

30. "The Frugal Shopper" is a publication co-authored by Ralph Nader, a leading consumer activist. Which of the following tips is NOT among the tips recommended?
    a. Consumers should avoid credit card insurance: price is high, benefits low.
    b. Consumers should avoid banks that charge for automated teller services. These services lower labor costs for banks. Why should you pay more?
    c. Consumers should avoid a loan with a prepayment penalty.
    d. Consumers should avoid energy-efficient appliances. Good for your pocketbook and the environment.

Note: Answers to the questions posed in this section appear in **PART III: Answers to Study Guide "Test Yourself" Questions** at the end of this *Study Guide*.

CHAPTER 5

MULTICULTURAL AND INTERNATIONAL MARKETING

CHAPTER SUMMARY

The United States is the world's most culturally diverse society. Marketers expect cultural differences in international markets, but they also face increasing cultural diversity in their own domestic market. Marketers need to develop understanding and sensitivity to cultural differences, while avoiding cultural myopia and the effects of the self-reference criteria. Marketers are culture change agents and must recognize how powerful marketing can be in speeding culture change.

The three largest ethnic microcultures in the United States are African-Americans, Hispanic-Americans, and Asian-Americans. Even though consumers may be identified with a microculture and group members may share some consumer preferences and behaviors, individual differences can be quite profound.

Businesses internationally market their products for a number of different reasons, sometimes because they experience unexpected foreign demand. Others follow key customers abroad in order to service them. The most common reasons for going international are to generate revenue, escape domestic competition, prolong product life, receive tax incentives, and dispose of discontinued goods. The ways that businesses go international are equally diverse. Entry strategies include direct and indirect exporting, joint ventures, wholly owned subsidiaries, licensing, and franchising.

Successful international marketers must consider environmental factors when planning and implementing marketing activities. Among the most important international environmental factors are culture, political and legal factors, and economic factors, including technology and level of economic development.

Three important contemporary international marketing issues involve the North American Free Trade Agreement (NAFTA), European integration, and the emergence of the Pacific Rim. All have implications for free trade and international competitiveness.

CHAPTER OBJECTIVES

This chapter is organized around a series of numbered learning objectives. Each objective statement that follows includes space for you to restate the statement as a question, then answer it with a concise answer that also summarizes the text section.

Step 1   Restate the objective statement as a question.

Step 2   Read the corresponding section in the textbook.

Step 3   Based on what you have read, answer the objective question.

CHAPTER OBJECTIVES

1. **Explain why marketers should develop cultural understanding.**

   Question

   Answer

129

2. Identify the three largest ethnic microcultures in the United States.

Question

Answer

3. Discuss how and why businesses go international.

Question

Answer

4. Describe the environment of international marketing.

Question

Answer

5. Analyze the contemporary issues facing international marketers.

Question

Answer

CHAPTER OUTLINE

I. Explain why marketers should develop cultural understanding.

.

.

.

.

.

.

II. Identify the three largest ethnic microcultures in the United States.

-
-
-
-
-

III. Discuss why and how businesses go international.

-
-
-
-

IV. Describe the environment of international marketing.

      .

      .

      .

      .

      .

      .

V. Analyze the contemporary issues facing international marketers.

      .

      .

      .

      .

KEY TERMS

In the space beside each key term, write your own definition of the term <u>without referring to the textbook.</u>

KEY TERMS FOR YOU TO DEFINE

Cultural Blinders

Culture

Socialization

Self-Reference Criterion

Culture Clash

Macroculture

Multicultural Society

Microculture

Values

Homogeneous

Heterogeneous

Cultural Sensitivity

Cultural Borrowing

Cultural Change

Domestic Marketing

International Marketing

Export

Import

Trade Deficit

Standard of Living

Gross Domestic Product (GDP)

Protectionism

Tariff

GATT

Indirect Exporting

Direct Exporting

Joint Venture

Direct Ownership

Global Marketing

Dumping

CHAPTER QUESTIONS AND ACTIVITIES

This section provides you with a place to answer the questions posed in the textbook in the **Check Your Understanding** sections and in the **Discussion Questions, Mini-Cases,** and **What Do You Think?** at the end of the chapter. Space is also provided for your reactions to **Marketing Applications, Consumer Insights, International Marketing,** and **Marketing on the Internet.**

CHECK YOUR UNDERSTANDING

■ **Check Your Understanding 5.1**

1. Compare and contrast the U.S. macro- with the principal U.S. and microcultures.

2. What is the self-reference criterion and why is it important?

3. Why is language an important element in culture?

■ **Check Your Understanding 5.2**

1. Define the term *cultural sensitivity* and explain its importance to marketers in a multicultural society.

2. Are marketers cultural change agents? Explain your answer.

3. Identify the largest ethnic microcultures in the United States and describe some of their characteristics.

■ **Check Your Understanding 5.3**

1. Why should businesses consider going international?

2. What kind of help can businesses get in going abroad?

3. What is the Triad? What are the emerging nations?

■ **Check Your Understanding 5.4**

1. Is international marketing more complex than domestic marketing?

2. What are some common barriers to entry?

3. What is global marketing?

■ **Check Your Understanding 5.5**

1. Discuss different product alternatives that can be offered to international markets.

2. Why is pricing more complex in international markets?

3. Describe the contemporary issues concerning international marketing.

MARKETING APPLICATIONS

■ **MARKETING APPLICATION 5.1**

What is the issue raised by this **Marketing Application**?

What conclusions can you draw from this activity about the use of core values in print advertisements? Do the values expressed in the advertisements reflect the core values identified in Figure 5.1 (page 141 of the text)?

■ MARKETING APPLICATION 5.2

What is the issue raised by this **Marketing Application**?

What conclusions can you draw from this activity about cultural borrowing of foods? What popular American foods have been exported?

■ MARKETING APPLICATION 5.3

What is the issue raised by this Marketing Application?

What conclusions can you draw from this activity about the involvement of American corporations in international marketing?

■ MARKETING APPLICATION 5.4

What is the issue raised by this **Marketing Application**?

What conclusions can you draw from this activity about sources for information and assistance in going international?

■ MARKETING APPLICATION 5.5

What is the issue raised by this **Marketing Application**?

What conclusions can you draw from this activity about the importance of learning about culture as an important element in an international marketing situation analysis?

DISCUSSION QUESTIONS

1. What are the three largest ethnic microcultures in the United States?

2. What is the difference between a macroculture and a microculture?

3. Explain what is meant by the term *multicultural society*.

4. What are American core values? Explain how they are used in describing a nation.

5. Compare and contrast the terms *homogeneous* and *heterogeneous*.

6. Do you think body language is important in marketing? Explain.

7. Can cultural sensitivity be overdone? Might it threaten the unity of the United States if immigrants don't assimilate?

8. Are marketers cultural change agents? Could this be the case even in the United States? Explain.

9. How are recent immigrants to the United States contributing to international marketing?

10. Why do businesses go international? Describe the important factors a marketer must consider when going international and selecting target markets.

MINI-CASES

■ **Mini-Case 5.1: Pier 1: Retailer of Global Goods Goes International.**

In your own words, summarize this case in the space below.

1. What do you think of Pier 1's plans? Is their strategy an example of "go global, think local?"

2. Would you recommend that Pier 1 find a local partner in the countries where it plans to open stores? Explain your answer.

3. Is the plan to market to Puerto Rico the same way Pier 1 markets to Florida a good one? Explain.

■ **Mini-Case 5.2: Joint Ventures at Home and Abroad**

In your own words, summarize this case in the space below.

1. What do you think of joint ventures? What are the benefits and shortcomings?

2. What can a catalog company gain from forming a joint venture partnership with a magazine targeted to African-American women?

3. What can AT&T gain from having joint venture partners in China?

WHAT DO YOU THINK?

*In your own words, summarize the issue addressed in this **WHAT DO YOU THINK?**, then answer the questions.*

. Do you think the human rights activists are right, that trade with China should be restricted until the Chinese government improves the way it treats its citizens?

. Is the road to democracy in China through economic reform and trade?

. Should American consumers boycott products made in China?

. In addition to the Chinese human rights problem, the Chinese government is also accused of turning a blind eye to massive product counterfeiting operations that reproduce music and video disks, computer programs, and other products without sharing profits with the product and copyright owners. The Chinese military is said to be involved in some of these operations. Considering these two problems, human rights violations and counterfeiting, should the United States government consider taking trade action against China? What are the risks of doing so?

CONSUMER INSIGHTS, INTERNATIONAL MARKETING

■ CONSUMER INSIGHT 5.1

What is the issue raised by this **Consumer Insight**?

■ CONSUMER INSIGHT 5.2

What is the issue raised by this **Consumer Insight**?

■ INTERNATIONAL MARKETING REPORT

What is the issue raised by this **International Marketing Report**?

MARKETING ON THE INTERNET

What is the issue raised by this **Marketing On The Internet**?

CHAPTER 5
TEST YOURSELF

The Chapter 5 opening question is

Will growing multicultural diversity in the United States affect the international marketing efforts of U.S. businesses?

What is your answer to this question now that you have completed reading the chapter?

■ TRUE OR FALSE

For each of the following questions, print T (true) or F (false) on the line beside the number.

_____ 1. By the year 2050, Asians, Hispanics, African-Americans, and other non-Caucasian groups could represent 47 percent of the total U.S. population.

_____ 2. The United States is a monocultural society, highly homogeneous and culturally uniform.

_____ 3. Japan's culture prizes individuality, entrepreneurship, and individual effort.

_____ 4. Language is one of the strongest forces unifying or separating communities.

_____ 5. Because of growing workforce diversity in the United States, greater cultural sensitivity is also required when marketing to business and organization consumers.

_____ 6. All cultures are willing and eager to borrow from one another.

_____ 7. Cultural change is accelerated through the marketing of licensed products in other countries.

_____ 8. Hispanic-Americans are the most rapidly growing U.S. microculture.

_____ 9. Dumping occurs when a foreign marketer sells products abroad at a price higher than the products are sold for in the marketer's home market or higher than the cost of production.

_____10. Because the Internet has no global boundaries, it has the potential to reduce or eliminate many differences between marketing domestically and internationally.

■ COMPLETION

Complete each sentence by filling-in-the-blank.

11. When a person's opinions about another culture are restricted to accepting only what their own culture considers acceptable so that they cannot see or readily accept other cultures' ways, that person is said to be wearing _____ _____.

12. _____ are the things a society holds in high esteem.

13. The characteristics of "generosity, helping your neighbors, being there in an emergency" reflect the American core value of _____.

14. It is estimated that 60 percent of all communication is nonverbal, through what is often called _____ language.

15. The stages of cultural perception begin with _____ and end in _____.

147

16. Currently, the largest American microculture is that of _____.

17. There are about 25 million _____ in the United States, a number slightly less than the population of Canada.

18. When a country has trade imports greater than exports, it is said to be running a _____ _____.

19. The Triad dominates world trade and is composed of _____, _____, and _____.

20. Markets that are developing, growing, and represent great potential are called _____ markets.

■ **MULTIPLE CHOICE**

Circle the letter of the best answer.

21. People learn culturally acceptable behaviors and attitudes through a process called ____.
    a. reeducation
    b. classification
    c. socialization
    d. deculturation

22. In a multicultural society, like the United States, people are members of the entire society, the _____ culture, and at the same time, are also members of one or more _____ cultures.
    a. macro; micro
    b. maxi; macro
    c. macro; main
    d. micro; mini

23. Which of the following is NOT a core American value as identified in Figure 5.1?
    a. Fitness and health.
    b. Activity.
    c. Youthfulness.
    d. Teamwork and cooperation.

24. Which of the following is a FALSE statement?
    a. The United States had few immigrants until the arrival of the first immigrant wave after World War II in the mid-1950s.
    b. Because of growing workforce diversity in the United States, greater cultural sensitivity is also needed when marketing to business and organization consumers.
    c. Miami has more foreign-born residents than any other major American city.
    d. Hispanics make up 49 percent of Dade County, Florida.

25. Leon has doubled his medical supplies business by selling products to distributors in England, the Netherlands, and Spain. He is offering finished products directly to markets in other nations through the process of ____.
    a. importing
    b. exporting
    c. reporting
    d. trading

26. There are many reasons why a business begins marketing internationally. Which of the following is NOT a frequently cited reason for going international?
    a. To generate revenue.
    b. To follow a major customer.
    c. To seek high risk markets.
    d. To receive tax incentives.

148

27. Many international marketers believe that the emerging markets represent great potential. Which of the following is an emerging market?
    a. Canada.
    b. China.
    c. Japan.
    d. England.

28. The country with the second largest land area in the world and the United States's best trading partner is ____.
    a. Canada
    b. China
    c. Japan
    d. Mexico

29. Marketing must generate revenues. Therefore, marketers target international markets where there are sufficient consumers to purchase their products. One economic measure that marketers may evaluate is a country's ____, a composite figure indicating the total value of the products produced annually by the country.
    a. Gross Domestic Product (GDP)
    b. Gross International Product (GIP)
    c. Standard of Living
    d. Trade Surplus

30. AT&T is entering into agreements around the world with other companies to market products internationally. This form of international marketing entry alternative is called ____.
    a. direct ownership
    b. indirect exporting
    c. direct venturing
    d. joint venture

Note: Answers to the questions posed in this section appear in **PART III: Answers to Study Guide "Test Yourself" Questions** at the end of this *Study Guide*.

CHAPTER 6
MARKETING RESEARCH AND INFORMATION TECHNOLOGY

CHAPTER SUMMARY

Chapter 6 looks at how important information is to marketers. Good information used wisely can help marketers recognize and take advantage of windows of opportunity, avoid threats, and achieve competitive advantage. Usable information must be current, reliable, suitable, sufficient, affordable, and available. Advances in computer technology have advanced the information revolution, which is affecting the way marketers collect and use information. While there are many benefits to the information revolution, there also are some hazards, including information overload and technology overkill.

Marketing is information-intensive. Marketers must have information to make good decisions involving the marketing mix variables, product, price, place, and promotion. They use both descriptive and prescriptive information. Marketers must manage information effectively in order to make decisions that satisfy consumers and achieve business goals.

A marketing information system (MIS) is an organized, systematic process designed to help marketers effectively manage and use information. Contemporary MIS systems integrate three sets of interrelated activities: information collection, information analysis, and information dissemination. Most MIS systems rely heavily on computers to aid in these activities.

Some use sophisticated computer-based systems called Marketing Decision Support Systems (MDSS) that rely on highly complex statistical programs to suggest answers to specific marketing problems.

Marketing research, according to the American Marketing Association, links the consumer, customer, and public to the marketer through information. Marketing research is a systematic process for establishing that link and facilitating the use of information in making marketing decisions. Research should be conducted when additional information is needed in marketing activities. Marketing research is performed by individuals and groups, in small, mid-size, and large businesses, as well as by businesses whose sole mission is to conduct research and sell the results. Marketing research generally follows a prescribed set of steps. Marketers strive to perform research that is valid, reliable, and generalizable.

In the last 30 years, the information revolution has accelerated. This is affecting marketing, as well as society and business generally. Electronic measuring devices, facsimile machines, virtual reality, and the Internet are just some examples of new technologies that are changing the ways that marketing activities are conducted.

CHAPTER OBJECTIVES

This chapter is organized around a series of numbered learning objectives. Each objective statement that follows includes space for you to restate the statement as a question, then answer it with a concise answer that also summarizes the text section.

Step 1   Restate the objective statement as a question.

Step 2   Read the corresponding section in the textbook.

Step 3   Based on what you have read, answer the objective question.

■ OBJECTIVES

1. Explain why information is so important to marketers.

Question

Answer

2. Understand that all marketers need information.

Question

Answer

3. Describe a marketing information system (MIS) and explain how it works.

Question

Answer

4. Identify the steps in marketing research.

   Question

   Answer

5. Discuss how recent advances in information technology are pushing marketing in new directions.

   Question

   Answer

CHAPTER OUTLINE

I. Explain why information is so important to marketers.

153

II. **Understand that all marketers need information.**

.

.

.

.

.

.

III. **Describe a marketing information system (MIS) and explain how it works.**

.

.

154

IV. Identify the steps in marketing research.

V. Discuss how recent advances in information technology are pushing marketing in new directions.

155

●

●

●

●

KEY TERMS

In the space beside each key term, write your own definition of the term <u>without referring to the textbook</u>.

■ **KEY TERMS FOR YOU TO DEFINE**

Information

Data

Hardware

Software

Descriptive Information

Prescriptive Information

Information Overload

Marketing Information System

Quantitative

Qualitative

Primary Data

Secondary Data

Workflow Automation

Market Research

Advertising Research

Consumer Behavior Research

Exploratory Research

Validity

Reliability

Generalizability

CHAPTER QUESTIONS AND ACTIVITIES

This section provides you with a place to answer the questions posed in the textbook in the **Check Your Understanding** sections and in the **Discussion Questions, Mini-Cases,** and **What Do You Think?** at the end of the chapter. Space is also provided for your reactions to **Marketing Applications, Consumer Insights, International Marketing,** and **Marketing on the Internet.**

CHECK YOUR UNDERSTANDING

■ **Check Your Understanding 6.1**

1. What is information and how is it used in marketing?

2. Explain this statement: "Marketing is information-intensive."

3. Why must marketers be concerned about managing information?

■ **Check Your Understanding 6.2**

1. Describe what takes place in a marketing information system.

2. Identify sources for information collected internally in an MIS.

3. Distinguish between commercial intelligence and espionage.

■ **Check Your Understanding 6.3**

1. What is marketing research? What are market and advertising research?

2. Identify the steps in marketing research.

3. Compare and contrast primary and secondary data/research.

MARKETING APPLICATIONS

■ MARKETING APPLICATION 6.1

What is the issue raised by this **Marketing Application**?

What conclusions can you draw from this activity about the need to define *what* information is needed before beginning to collect it? How effective is brainstorming as a technique used to define information types?

■ MARKETING APPLICATION 6.2

What is the issue raised by this **Marketing Application**?

What conclusions can you draw from this activity about the availability of information?

■ **MARKETING APPLICATION 6.3**

What is the issue raised by this **Marketing Application**?

What conclusions can you draw from this activity about the usefulness of surveys in collecting information? What are some of the advantages and disadvantages of conducting survey research?

DISCUSSION QUESTIONS

1. Explain this statement: "We are in the midst of an information explosion."

2. What do computers have to do with the information explosion?

3. Distinguish between computer hardware and software.

4. Explain what is meant by the term marketing information system.

5. Describe the three common sources of information collected by marketers.

6. Contrast primary and secondary data, and primary and secondary research.

7. Describe the steps in marketing research.

8. What three research considerations are very important to the marketer and underlie his or her confidence in research results?

9. Why are customer surveys such a popular form of marketing research?

10. What are some of the new technologies affecting marketing?

161

MINI-CASES

■ **Mini-Case 6.1: Vons Does it the Customers' Way**

In your own words, summarize this case in the space below.

1. Could the Vons approach be used in *all* supermarkets?

2. Could Vons carry this customization process too far? Explain your answer.

3. Are there any consumer privacy issues involved in this case? Explain your answer.

■ **Mini-Case 6.2: Marketing Research Serves Different Needs**

In your own words, summarize this case in the space below.

1. Many churches are using marketing research, advertisements, and direct marketing to reach their markets. Do you think there is any opposition to churches using marketing? What might be the basis for this opposition?

2. If a church decides to use a marketing research survey to determine its market's preferences, who should be surveyed? Should only current members be questioned? Explain your answer.

WHAT DO YOU THINK?

In your own words, summarize the issue addressed in this WHAT DO YOU THINK?, then answer the questions.

. What do you think about the Japanese approach to research? Do you think this approach is also being used in the United States?

CONSUMER INSIGHTS, INTERNATIONAL MARKETING

■ **CONSUMER INSIGHT 6.1**

What is the issue raised by this **Consumer Insight**?

■ INTERNATIONAL MARKETING REPORT

What is the issue raised by this **International Marketing Report**?

MARKETING ON THE INTERNET

What is the issue raised by this **Marketing On The Internet**?

CHAPTER 6
TEST YOURSELF

The Chapter 6 opening question is

How can information be used by marketers to gain competitive advantage?

What is your answer to this question now that you have completed reading the chapter?

■ TRUE OR FALSE

For each of the following questions, print T (true) or F (false) on the line beside the number.

____ 1. Marketers are told repeatedly that they don't have to worry about satisfying customers because there are so many customers that even if some become dissatisfied, there are always others to replace them.

____ 2. Often the terms data and information are used interchangeably.

____ 3. Hardware is a term used to describe computer programs such as spreadsheets, word processors, and database managers.

____ 4. The top information need of marketing managers is for information that can be used in improving new product development.

____ 5. Descriptive information describes something, for example what styles of winter clothing male consumers ages 25 to 35 are *buying*.

____ 6. The Internet has been a disappointment so far because so little information is available there for retrieval.

____ 7. Because scanner data are collected infrequently, they are considered an example of nonroutine information collection.

____ 8. An MDSS (Marketing Delivery Service System) is an accelerated process for delivering purchased goods.

____ 9. Marketing research links the consumer, customer, and public to the marketer through information.

____ 10. Some of the giant U.S. marketing research companies are expanding rapidly into international markets.

■ COMPLETION

Complete each sentence by filling-in-the-blank.

11. Information _____ occurs when the mass of information and its disorganization is overwhelming and instead of helping marketers make good decisions, it threatens good decision making.

12. Marketers often work together with computer hardware and various programs, to manage information so that it can be used efficiently in making marketing decisions. This system is often referred to as a marketing _____ _____ (MIS).

13. Joshi is involved in collecting data specifically to resolve a question about consumer preferences for shampoo. She is collecting _____ data.

14. As part of his job, Mark routinely collects company accounting records, daily sales receipts, weekly expense records and profit statements, production and shipment schedules, inventory records, orders, monthly credit statements, and quarterly and biennial reports to use as input information in his company's MIS. These routinely collected information sources are all considered _____ _____ information.

15. Carola is at the first step in her marketing research project. This means that she has to _____ the _____.

16. Research that is conducted in order to search for information that will help redefine or clarify the problem is called _____ research.

17. Sherrill is very concerned about survey _____. This means that she is being very careful to ask the right questions and collect the right information to ensure that the survey she is designing will measure what she is trying to measure.

18. Jock, a marketer for Kiddie Care Centers, USA, is running a _____ group with a group of women professionals, trying to determine the depth and nature of their concerns about child care. This is a group research interview with 8 to 12 participants, led by a moderator who guides the discussion.

19. Missy, a clerk at Little Red's Grocery, is running a check-out _____. These devices are used in 80 percent of U.S. supermarkets and 50 percent of retail stores, and capture such purchase information as brand names, manufacturer, size, price, and often, purchaser identification.

20. _____ reality systems are sophisticated 3-dimensional computer-generated images that made their first appearance in arcade games and are now being used in business applications.

■ MULTIPLE CHOICE

Circle the letter of the best answer.

21. Mark has collected large amounts of information to use in his company's MIS system. He knows that in order for information to be of value, it must be
    a. useful, affordable, available, and sufficient.
    b. useful, current, suitable, sufficient, affordable, and available.
    c. good.
    d. affordable, suitable, and current.

22. Sherrill uses a computer to perform spreadsheet calculations. Sherrill is using it as a(an) ____.
    a. electronic ledger
    b. clip art model
    c. printshop
    d. electronic mail router

23. Tommy has read an article that identifies the ways that marketing managers use the information that they collect. Which of the following was NOT identified as one of the top 10 ways that marketing managers use information?
    a. To improve the use of market information.
    b. In market segmentation and implementation activities.
    c. To identify strategic new product issues.
    d. To develop electronic mail and entertainment systems.

24. Stacey is collecting descriptive information about a group of consumers. This means that she is interested in what these consumers ____.
    a. feel, perceive, think
    b. feel, buy, return
    c. do, perceive, feel, say
    d. do, buy, say

25. Tod is looking at some computer software that will help him manage the mass of information he has to analyze as part of a marketing research project. This help desk software is also called
    a. electronic assistants.
    b. navigators.
    c. search tools.
    d. CEOs.

26. Part of Mark's job is to help compile the company's semiannual report. Because this report is published twice yearly, this frequency identifies it as a form of ____ information collection.
    a. routine
    b. periodic
    c. nonroutine
    d. irregular

27. A marketing information system (MIS) is a three-step process of activities that includes information integration. Information integration requires
    a. collecting internal company information, external information, and conducting marketing research.
    b. directing information to the right decision makers.
    c. classifying, sorting, analyzing, retrieving, and synthesizing information.
    d. deciding what the problem is, stating it, conducting exploratory research to better refine the research question.

28. Subjective information, such as the information collected by salespeople, summaries of conversations with consumers, analyzes of competitors' actions are called ____ information.
    a. quantitative
    b. exploratory
    c. investigative
    d. qualitative

29. Erik is conducting research on such things as ad and copy effectiveness, recall, and media choice. This type of research is classified as ____ research.
    a. consumer behavior
    b. market
    c. advertising
    d. sales

30. Which of the following is NOT a commonly identified step in marketing research?
    a. Identify the problem.
    b. Implement an MDSS system.
    c. Collect the information.
    d. Report findings and recommendations.

Note: Answers to the questions posed in this section appear in PART III: Answers to Study Guide "Test Yourself" Questions at the end of this *Study Guide*.

CHAPTER 7

UNDERSTANDING PRODUCT

CHAPTER SUMMARY

A product is anything offered to buyers to satisfy their wants and needs in exchange for something of value. It is a complex bundle of benefits and a focal point for decisions involving the other marketing mix variables of price, place, and promotion. Marketers use the marketing mix variables to differentiate their products from others and establish a competitive advantage. Products are classified in order to promote understanding, establish relationships, and determine how successful marketing strategies can be used for similar products. Two important product classifications are used to identify the nature of products (goods and services) and product target markets (personal use and business/organization consumers).

Products can be thought of as being composed of three parts. The core is the basic product. The augmented (or extended) product is what the consumer expects beyond the core and the seller adds to make the core product more attractive and to differentiate it from the competition. The potential product is what might be added to further enhance the product and add to the value of the product for consumers.

Many different individuals and groups hold important views about products and their perspectives affect product marketing. Government views product as something to be monitored to ensure consumer safety and free market competition. The competition views product as something to closely observe, sometimes dissect and copy, and as a potential threat to their product's profitability. The members of a product's distribution system view product as their reason for being and source of profit. Within a business, product can elicit differing and sometimes opposing views. To the consumer, product satisfies needs and fulfills wants.

Marketers must make a number of important decisions about products. These decisions contribute to the development of a product strategy. This includes decisions about product features, lines and mixes, quality, design, branding, legal protection, packaging, labeling, and at the end of the product life cycle, the product termination decision.

Legal protection is essential to defend product assets. Packaging protects goods physically, as well as contributes to product image and promotion. A label provides information that consumers need to make informed product decisions.

CHAPTER OBJECTIVES

This chapter is organized around a series of numbered learning objectives. Each objective statement that follows includes space for you to restate the statement as a question, then answer it with a concise answer that also summarizes the text section.

Step 1   Restate the objective statement as a question.

Step 2   Read the corresponding section in the textbook.

Step 3   Based on what you have read, answer the objective question.

■ CHAPTER OBJECTIVES

1. Recognize the nature of product.

Question

Answer

2. Describe the total product concept.

Question

Answer

3. Identify different perspectives on product.

Question

Answer

4. Explain the issues involved in making product decisions.

Question

Answer

5. Describe how product assets are protected.

Question

Answer

CHAPTER OUTLINE

I. Recognize the nature of product.

- .

- .

- .

- .

II. Describe the total product concept.

-

-

-

-

-

-

III. Identify different perspectives on product.

-

-

IV. Explain the issues involved in making product decisions.

V. Describe how product assets are protected.

·

·

·

·

KEY TERMS

In the space beside each key term, write your own definition of the term <u>without referring to the textbook</u>.

■ **KEY TERMS FOR YOU TO DEFINE**

Product Differentiation

Goods

Durable Goods

Nondurable Goods

Services

Industrial Products

Augmented Products

Potential Product

Product Strategy

Product Line

Product Category

Product Mix

Width

Depth

Image

Design

Brand

Brand Name

Brand Mark

Service Mark

Brand Equity

Brand Loyalty

National (Manufacturer's) Brand

Store Brand (Private Label)

Mixed Branding

Brand Extension

Cobranding

Cannibalizing

SUGGESTED QUESTIONS AND ACTIVITIES

This section provides you with a place to answer the questions posed in the textbook in the **Check Your Understanding** sections and in the **Discussion Questions, Mini-Cases,** and **What Do You Think?** at the end of the chapter. Space is also provided for your reactions to **Marketing Applications, Consumer Insights, International Marketing,** and **Marketing on the Internet.**

CHECK YOUR UNDERSTANDING

■ **Check Your Understanding 7.1**

1. Explain this statement: "The T-shirt is the Big Mac of the international clothing industry." Do you agree or disagree?

2. Provide your own definition of *product*.

3. Distinguish between the nature of goods and services, and personal use and business/organization products.

■ **Check Your Understanding 7.2**

1. What is the core product?

2. What is the augmented product?

3. What is the potential product?

    1. What product perspective should a business take? Explain your answer.

    2. What is the government's perspective on product?

    3. Explain why there may be different perspectives on product within a business. Why might this result in conflict?

    1. Discuss the types of product decisions that must be made.

    2. Explain the difference between national manufacturer's branding and store branding.

3. Discuss the difficulty of defining quality.

■ **Check Your Understanding 7.5**

1. Why is it important to protect product assets?

2. Why is packaging often called the "last five seconds of marketing?"

3. What does a label do for consumers?

MARKETING APPLICATIONS

■ **MARKETING APPLICATION 7.1**

What is the issue raised by this **Marketing Application**?

What conclusions can you draw from this activity about the difficulty of identifying the consumer problem that a product is designed to solve?

■ MARKETING APPLICATION 7.2

What is the issue raised by this **Marketing Application**?

What conclusions can you draw from this activity about how important it is to design products that are user-friendly?

■ MARKETING APPLICATION 7.3

What is the issue raised by this **Marketing Application**?

What conclusions can you draw from this activity about the importance of quality to consumers and the differences in their perceptions about product quality?

■ MARKETING APPLICATION 7.4

What is the issue raised by this **Marketing Application**?

What conclusions can you draw from this activity about the difficulty of selecting the right name for a product?

■ MARKETING APPLICATION 7.5

What is the issue raised by this **Marketing Application**?

What conclusions can you draw from this activity about the new product labels? Are they informative? Are they easy to read and understand?

DISCUSSION QUESTIONS

1. Explain the concept of product as core, extended, and augmented parts.

2. Identify some tools used to differentiate products.

3. Why is it important to distinguish among various types of products?

4. Describe Copeland's classification system and explain its importance to a marketer.

5. Discuss the types of product decisions that a marketer must make. Are all of the decisions made solely by marketers? Explain.

6. What is a product line? Give an example of one.

7. Compare and contrast: product line, product category, product mix.

181

8. What is value? Why is it important to the consumer? To the marketer?

9. If you were marketing national manufacturer's brands, how might you feel about private-label brands?

10. What is cobranding?

MINI-CASES

■ **Mini-Case 7.1: The Best Brand In The World?**

In your own words, summarize this case in the space below.

1. What value is there to a brand in being named to a top 10 list like EquiTrend's?

2. Explain Coca-Cola's popularity worldwide.

3. Discuss possible meanings for the statement, "Coca-Cola is the *best brand* in the world.

■ **Mini-Case 7.2: Buyers and Marketers Beware: Fakes Flood Markets**

In your own words, summarize this case in the space below.

1. Who should bear the responsibility for defective fake products - the owner of the brand name or the counterfeiter?

2. Why might some consumers want product counterfeiting to continue?

3. What, if anything, can governments do to stop the flow of counterfeit products?

WHAT DO YOU THINK?

In your own words, summarize the issue addressed in this WHAT DO YOU THINK?, then answer the questions.

. Is more of a product always better? Explain your answer.

. What are some drawbacks to having 500 television channels?

CONSUMER INSIGHTS, INTERNATIONAL MARKETING

■ CONSUMER INSIGHT 7.1

What is the issue raised by this **Consumer Insight**?

■ CONSUMER INSIGHT 7.2

What is the issue raised by this **Consumer Insight**?

■ **INTERNATIONAL MARKETING REPORT**

What is the issue raised by this **International Marketing Report**?

MARKETING ON THE INTERNET

What is the issue raised by this **Marketing On The Internet**?

185

CHAPTER 7
TEST YOURSELF

The Chapter 7 opening question is

What product opportunities will emerge in the next century?

What is your answer to this question now that you have completed reading the chapter?

■ TRUE OR FALSE

For each of the following questions, print T (true) or F (false) on the line beside the number.

____ 1. While services are important to marketers, only tangible goods are classified as products.

____ 2. Branding is one method used to help differentiate products.

____ 3. A refrigerator, a long lasting good that is replaced only infrequently, is classified as a non-durable good.

____ 4. Copeland's product classification system is based on buyer habits, the consumer's view of the product, where, and how it is purchased.

____ 5. At this point in the evolution of the Internet, the only products being sold on the World Wide Web are computer hardware and software.

____ 6. Martin Shine, Inc., a small cable box manufacturer, is considered an industrial products purchaser of goods and services.

____ 7. Burial plots and caskets are classified as unsought personal use consumer products.

____ 8. What a product appears to be depends to a great extent on whose product perspective is taken.

____ 9. It isn't always clear what consumer problem a product is designed to solve.

____10. In production, quality refers to zero defects or conformity to exact manufacturing and production specifications.

■ COMPLETION

Complete each sentence by filling-in-the-blank.

11. An issue of growing concern to many consumers and environmentalists is the use of excessive product packaging, also known as _____.

12. There are four approaches to protecting product assets _____, copyrights, _____, and trade secret protection.

13. Lawson Co. is about ready to launch a new product, Terrific Tom Tomato Juice With Hot Sauce. Marketing managers are somewhat anxious because they anticipate the new product may actually steal market share from the company's existing tomato juice products, in other words, _____ existing products.

14. Adding the up-scale Avalon to the Toyota product line is an example of a brand _____.

186

15. DAX Stores uses its own name on many of the products that it sells. This is an example of the use of a private label or _____ brand.

16. A _____ has been called "a company's most important asset."

17. _____ is how a product appears to the customer through such details as colors, use of symbols, packaging, displays, price, and how and where it is sold and advertised.

18. The Delta Company's Product Development group is planning how the Company will bring its new line of action toys to market. The planning required to bring a new product from the idea stage to commercialization is part of the development of a product _____.

19. In planning for the commercialization of a new line of liquid dish washing detergents, the Product Development group is also considering what might be added in the future to increase the value of the product to consumers. Two of their ideas are for adding antibacterial agents and hand softening lotions. This interest in what might be added to the product in the future concerns the _____ part of the total product.

20. Products that are easily accessible, familiar, and frequently purchased according to Copeland's classification system are _____ products.

■ MULTIPLE CHOICE

Circle the letter of the best answer.

21. Some products are mass produced with few if any variations offered while others are ____ to satisfy particular consumers.
    a. customized
    b. accessibilized
    c. cannibalized
    d. classified

22. Products that are frequently replaced, such as laundry detergents, food perishables, and faddish clothing are classified as ____.
    a. nondurable services
    b. durable services
    c. nondurable goods
    d. durable goods

23. Which of the following is an example of a pure service?
    a. Haircut.
    b. Automobile rental.
    c. Notebook paper.
    d. Cellular telephone.

24. Peter is getting ready for his wedding day. Usually he just dashes into the local barber shop and gets the standard seven dollar buzz cut. But, because this is such a special day, he has decided to shop around and find a salon that will style his hair so he will look really good in the wedding pictures. This is an example of a consumer making a purchase of a ____ service.
    a. convenience
    b. shopping
    c. unsought
    d. specialty

25. Jessie is in the market for the fine oak wood that her company uses in constructing the Shaker furniture which they make using hand tools and sell at craft fairs around the country. Jessie is a business consumer making a purchase of ____.
    a. durable services
    b. capital items
    c. materials/parts
    d. core goods

26. There are many different perspectives on product. The ___ takes the perspective of monitoring product to ensure consumer safety and the perpetuation of the free market.
    a. members of the distribution channel
    b. government
    c. competition
    d. consumer

27. There are many different perspectives on product even within a company. For example, ____ people may take the perspective that product should primarily be a matter of functional and aesthetic issues.
    a. marketing
    b. design
    c. finance
    d. production

28. Which two countries are the only ones that have not completely converted over to the metric system of meters, grams, and liters?
    a. Canada and Mexico.
    b. China and Thailand.
    c. United States and Liberia.
    d. South Africa and Egypt.

29. All of a business's product offer, everything it brings to exchange with consumers, is the business's product ____.
    a. mix
    b. line
    c. category
    d. width

30. Merl wants value in a product. When he purchases a new lawn mower, he is going to look for value by comparing different mowers primarily on their relative ____.
    a. price, quality, and image
    b. brand and quality
    c. quality and design
    d. image, brand, and design

Note: Answers to the questions posed in this section appear in **PART III: Answers to Study Guide "Test Yourself" Questions** at the end of this *Study Guide*.

CHAPTER 8

PRODUCT PROCESSES

CHAPTER SUMMARY

New products often are called the lifeblood of a company. However, newness is a matter of perspective. A product may be new to the business offering it, to consumers, an industry, or even a country. Product newness is often classified according to whether the product is revolutionary, evolutionary, or somewhere between the two. Product strategies are developed to try to assure that products achieve the business goals set for them. Some frequently used product strategies are to revitalize existing products, extend them, acquire new products, duplicate existing products, cooperate with others to jointly develop products, and generate new products through research and development processes.

Some businesses spend millions on research and the development of new products in the hope that they will gain profits, market leadership, and a competitive advantage. New product development typically proceeds through a series of steps. In some cases, consumers are involved with new product development from the start of the process. Development steps include opportunity scanning, idea generation, idea screening, concept testing, market analysis and marketing plan development, product production, test marketing, and commercialization. Product development requires teamwork. New product failure rates are high and as a result, some businesses are taking aggressive steps to make sure their products don't fail.

It is important for marketers to understand and describe consumer responses to products. The product adoption process describes how consumers proceed from first becoming aware of a new product to the point when they make a product purchase. Innovations diffuse through a society, with some consumers rushing to be among the first to purchase a new product, while the majority hold back, waiting to see how well the product is accepted by others before they adopt it. The product life cycle is a descriptive device for characterizing generally how consumers respond to products over time. The international product life cycle model suggests that product life cycles can be extended by introducing a product to international markets where it may be new, even as the same product is maturing or declining in the home market. Product positioning is another important consumer response that explains how consumers mentally perceive products and compare them on valued features. Sometimes a product must be repositioned, often because the initial consumer positioning was unfavorable or in response to changes in the competition or environment.

Once a product is launched, it must be managed in order to gain and sustain profitability. No single form of product management is effective for all businesses or products. Some businesses use brand managers, others use category managers, or form business groups to manage products.

Some important contemporary product issues confronting marketers are complaints. These complaints include concern about planned product obsolescence, consumer rights, product recalls, and product liability.

CHAPTER OBJECTIVES

This chapter is organized around a series of numbered learning objectives. Each objective statement that follows includes space for you to restate the statement as a question, then answer it with a concise answer that also summarizes the text section.

Step 1   Restate the objective statement as a question.

Step 2   Read the corresponding section in the textbook.

Step 3   Based on what you have read, answer the objective question.

CHAPTER OBJECTIVES

1. Explain how businesses obtain products.

Question

Answer

2. Characterize the new product development process and explain the importance of new products.

Question

Answer

3. Recognize the methods used to describe consumer responses to products.

Question

Answer

4. Compare different product management strategies.

Question

Answer

5. Identify contemporary product issues.

Question

Answer

CHAPTER OUTLINE

I. Explain how businesses obtain products.

-

-

-

-

-

-

II. Characterize the new product development process and explain the importance of new products.

-

-

-

-

-

III. Recognize the methods used to describe consumer responses to products.

-

192

IV. Compare different product management strategies.

193

V. Identify contemporary product issues.

•

•

•

•

•

•

KEY TERMS

In the space beside each key term, write your own definition of the term <u>without referring to the textbook</u>.

■ **KEY TERMS FOR YOU TO DEFINE**

Continuous Product Innovations

Discontinuous Product Innovations

Dynamically Continuous Product Innovations

Test Market

Product Adoption Process

Diffusion of Innovations

Product Life Cycle (PLC)

Perceptual Maps

Repositioning

Brand Manager

Category Manager

Business Group

CHAPTER QUESTIONS AND ACTIVITIES

This section provides you with a place to answer the questions posed in the textbook in the **Check Your Understanding** sections and in the **Discussion Questions, Mini-Cases,** and **What Do You Think?** at the end of the chapter. Space is also provided for your reactions to **Marketing Applications, Consumer Insights, International Marketing,** and **Marketing on the Internet.**

CHECK YOUR UNDERSTANDING

■ **Check Your Understanding 8.1**

1. Why are new products called the "lifeblood of a company?"

2. Explain this statement: "Newness is a matter of perspective."

3. Discuss the different ways a business may obtain products.

■ Check Your Understanding 8.2

1. Identify the steps in the new product development process and explain what happens in each step.

■ Check Your Understanding 8.3

1. What advantages do multifunctional development teams have in the development of new products?

2. Provide several explanations for why products fail.

3. What steps can be taken to ensure product success?

■ Check Your Understanding 8.4

1. Describe the product adoption process.

2. What is the product life cycle?

3. Explain the concept of product positioning and repositioning.

1. Why do products need to be managed?

2. Discuss the difference between a brand manager and a category manager.

3. Identify several contemporary product issues.

MARKETING APPLICATIONS

■ **MARKETING APPLICATION 8.1**

What is the issue raised by this **Marketing Application**?

What conclusions can you draw from this activity about "newness" in your selected product categories? How new are these products?

■ MARKETING APPLICATION 8.2

What is the issue raised by this **Marketing Application**?

What conclusions can you draw from this activity about look-alike products? Are there advantages for the consumer who buys a cheaper mirror product by mistake, uses it, and finds it works as well as the national manufacturer's branded product?

■ MARKETING APPLICATION 8.3

What is the issue raised by this **Marketing Application**?

What conclusions can you draw from this activity about product adoption patterns? What factors can influence whether or not a consumer is an early adopter?

■ **MARKETING APPLICATION 8.4**

What is the issue raised by this **Marketing Application**?

What conclusions can you draw from this activity about how consumer positioning of products compare? Use the positioning grid below to work **Marketing Application 8.4.**

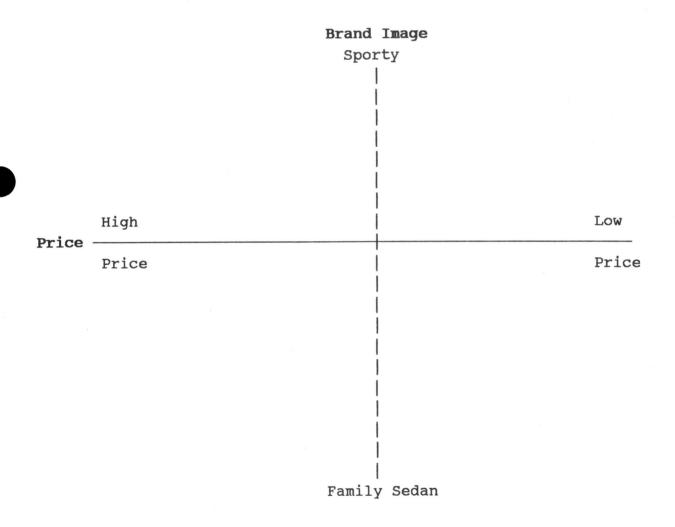

DISCUSSION QUESTIONS

1. Why is product newness a matter of perspective?

2. Compare and contrast the three levels of product newness.

3. What are the ways businesses obtain products?

4. Why would a business copy other businesses' products?

5. Describe the product strategy with the greatest inherent risk.

6. Compare and contrast idea generation and idea screening.

7. How are product concepts tested?

8. What is a test market?

9. Why do so many new products fail? What can be done to reverse this trend?

10. Compare and contrast such consumer responses to products as adoption, diffusion, and positioning.

MINI-CASES

■ **Mini-Case 8.1: Gillette's "Sensor for Women" Takes a Big Slice of the Market**

In your own words, summarize this case in the space below.

1. Most new products "wear out" after a relatively short time, particularly when their reign as market leader is threatened by knockoff me-too products. What can Gillette do to extend the success of the Sensor for Women and repel knockoffs?

2. If a *brand* life cycle were drawn for Sensor for Women, what stage would it be in? Explain your answer.

3. Considering the brand's market share, where is it in both the adoption and diffusion of innovations processes?

■ **Mini-Case 8.2: Brands Have Personalities, Too**

In your own words, summarize this case in the space below.

1. Why should a brand's personality be managed? What might happen if it were not managed correctly?

2. Brands are also associated with colors. Can you think of some brands that are associated with certain colors?

3. For each of the following brands, think of one adjective that describes the brand's personality (use stream-of-consciousness thoughts to select the first adjective that pops into your mind): Coca-Cola, Jell-O, Mr. Coffee, Betty Crocker, IBM, Apple Computer, and Disney.

WHAT DO YOU THINK?

In your own words, summarize the issue addressed in this WHAT DO YOU THINK?, then answer the questions.

. What do you think are P&G's chances for success with luxury products? What might the company do to try to assure its success?

CONSUMER INSIGHTS, INTERNATIONAL MARKETING

■ CONSUMER INSIGHT 8.1

What is the issue raised by this Consumer Insight?

■ CONSUMER INSIGHT 8.2

What is the issue raised by this **Consumer Insight**?

■ INTERNATIONAL MARKETING REPORT

What is the issue raised by this **International Marketing Report**?

MARKETING ON THE INTERNET

What is the issue raised by this **Marketing On The Internet**?

CHAPTER 8

TEST YOURSELF

The Chapter 8 opening question is

If new products are so crucial to business success (if not survival), why do so many of them fail despite efforts to ensure their success?

What is your answer to this question now that you have completed reading the chapter?

■ TRUE OR FALSE

For each of the following questions, print T (true) or F (false) on the line beside the number.

_____ 1. Because of the high rate of new product failures, marketers no longer call new products the lifeblood of a company.

_____ 2. A brand may be new, although the product itself is not.

_____ 3. Most new products are continuous innovations.

_____ 4. Marketers ignore a fad at their own risk, because even a short-term popular fad can result in considerable profit to early market entrants.

_____ 5. When Coca-Cola stretched its popular brand name to include Diet Coke, then Caffeine Free Coke and Cherry Coke, it was using a revitalization product strategy.

_____ 6. Most products offered on the Internet are not new, instead the Internet presents a new and different way of marketing existing products.

_____ 7. There are very few copycat products on the market.

_____ 8. Joint ventures are declining in popularity because companies don't want to share profits with others.

_____ 9. Opportunity scanning is the first step in product development.

_____10. New product development teams never consult with suppliers, wholesalers, or retailers because these members of the channel of distribution rarely are able to provide new product ideas.

■ COMPLETION

Complete each sentence by filling-in-the-blank.

11. Frito-Lay expanded its product line into popcorn when it made a deal to _____ Smart Food Popcorn Co.

12. The Crispy Chip Co. wants to see whether or not consumers will like their new fat-free baked potato chip. They have decided to sell the chip in two different cities for a limited time and carefully track consumer acceptance. The Crispy Chip Co. is going to run a _____ market.

13. The culmination of the new product development process is the product launch. This is also called _____.

14. Marion has just noticed that Office Depot is stocking a new office machine that is a combination printer, copier, and fax machine. Marion is in the _____ stage of the product adoption process.

15. Pop Rocks, hard candies that pop in your mouth, became popular very quickly and just as quickly disappeared from the market. This means the product was a _____.

16. Warp Software, Inc. will begin selling its new entertainment software in two weeks. This means that their new product is still in the _____ phase of the product life cycle.

17. Plots of how consumers perceive different products or brands in relation to one another are called _____ maps.

18. When Ford Motors found that demand for their new Contour automobile wasn't as high as expected, they blamed the poor sales on consumer perceptions. As a result, the car was relaunched with a new advertising campaign designed to _____ the car more favorably in consumers' minds.

19. Shawn is a _____ manager, which means that he manages the entire line of all the different branded frozen dinner products made by Swan's Frozen Foods, Inc.

20. Safety-Snap Baby Swings initiated a voluntary nationwide product _____ when it found that a defective part had been installed in its toddler swing set, and if the part broke it could cause the swing to collapse and hurt the user.

■ MULTIPLE CHOICE

Circle the letter of the best answer.

21. My computer is a 386 SX. I am about ready to invest in a new 486 DX computer. The new machine differs from the old one only in its greater storage space, because the 486 has a faster computer chip. The 486 DX computer is an example of a
    a. Dramatically continuous product innovation.
    b. Dynamically continuous product innovation.
    c. Discontinuous product innovation.
    d. Continuous product innovation.

22. The marketing mix variables are often used strategically to achieve product goals. Product promotion strategies designed to increase sales without changing the product may involve
    a. More advertising, different sales promotions, direct mailings.
    b. Increasing the number of places where the product is offered.
    c. Raising the product price.
    d. Lowering the product price.

23. Léon is talking to his company's salespeople and customers, gathering their observations and opinions about new products they would like the company to offer in its office product line. Léon is in the ____ step of product development.
    a. opportunity scanning
    b. idea screening
    c. concept testing
    d. test marketing

24. Félix, Léon, and Andrea are using the information Léon obtained, from talking to the company's salespeople and customers, to produce product ideas. Their goal is to produce as many ideas as possible, making creative leaps, piggybacking ideas, and not judging them for their feasibility. They are in the ___ step of product development.
   a. opportunity screening
   b. idea screening
   c. idea generation
   d. concept testing

25. Marcy is in the Richmond Mall, stopping every fifth woman shopper, age 25 to 35 years, who walks by, asking if they will help with a consumer survey. Most are willing to spend four minutes with Marcy. She shows each shopper a visual representation of the revolutionary new ladies' shaver her company is developing and describes how this product works. She collects demographic and product usage information from each shopper and determines whether or not they would be interested in purchasing this new, revolutionary product. Marcy is in the ___ step of product development.
   a. commercialization
   b. idea screening
   c. concept testing
   d. test marketing

26. Everything indicates that its new Taffy doll will be well received by its target market, so the Tooter Toy Company is going ahead with its launch of the product. Tooter Toy Co. is in the ____ step of product development.
   a. test marketing
   b. commercialization
   c. product production
   d. concept testing

27. Which of the following is NOT a typical reason given for the high failure rate of new products?
   a. Poor product quality.
   b. High product price.
   c. Bad timing.
   d. Uniqueness.

28. Gohary is strolling through the Richmond Mall, looking in the store windows as she walks. She is attracted to a display for a new jewelry cleaning compound that cleans fine jewelry using sonic waves. Gohary had never before seen such a product. She is in the ___ stage of the product adoption process.
   a. awareness
   b. interest
   c. evaluation.
   d. trial

29. Tide has been a market leader for decades, sustaining its revenues and profitability with little chance, even though many competitors have entered the market. Tide is in the ___ stage of the product life cycle.
   a. growth
   b. maturity
   c. introduction
   d. decline

30. Consumers showed very quickly that they didn't think the newly launched mouthwash was better than existing products. As a result, product sales were very disappointing. The mouthwash's brand manager and her team knew that they had to work fast to change their advertising and promotions to help consumers perceive the mouthwash in a new light. They are attempting to _____ the mouthwash.
    a. launch
    b. relaunch
    c. position
    d. reposition

Note: Answers to the questions posed in this section appear in **PART III: Answers to Study Guide "Test Yourself" Questions** at the end of this *Study Guide*.

CHAPTER 9

UNDERSTANDING PRICE

CHAPTER SUMMARY

Price is known by many different names and there are many different perspectives on it. Concern about price has risen in the past several decades, fueled by changes in the economic environment, swings in consumer confidence, and increased price competition domestically and internationally. Consumer confidence, an important indicator of future purchase behaviors, has obvious price implications. When consumers are not confident of their jobs and futures, their spending usually declines. Because consumers have become more price sensitive, marketers must consider this in their pricing decisions.

The many different perspectives on price also affect pricing decisions. Consumers often perceive price as a surrogate for value cues. Some consumers are price conscious, others are not. Consumers make price comparisons between products, using this information in their purchase decisions. Price is an allocation device, rationing products among consumers and balancing supply and demand. For most products, the law of demand holds so that price and demand move in opposite directions. For essential products, inelastic demand prevails so that a change in price does not have the expected effect on demand. Because these products are necessities, consumers will continue to purchase them (up to a point) even when prices are raised. A marketer must be aware of the various perspectives on price, including those of the government, consumers, the business, the competition, and channel of distribution members.

Other price influences are costs, the economy, seasons, special events, nature, and suppliers.

Good information, collected from internal and external sources, is essential to making good price decisions. Some price decisions follow the market leader's prices, other decisions include those that are based on tradition, judgment, an industry standard, or statistical forecasts. Pricing decisions generally follow four steps: setting price objectives, formulating a pricing strategy, setting price tactics, and making price adjustments, if and as needed.

Prices change as a result of the influence of many different factors. Marketers use a variety of pricing approaches, including odd/even, loss leader, bundled, prestige, time-period, and trial pricing that are designed to serve different marketing goals. Most marketers will tell you that pricing is both an art and a science. While many marketers use statistical models and computer simulations to help set prices, often the final price is determined with considerable input from experienced marketers who have developed a sense of what the market will tolerate. There is a place for objective, statistical, and subjective judgmental input to price decisions.

Price is a critical marketing mix variable and the one that most directly and quickly affects revenue. However, price cannot be considered apart from the other marketing mix variables (product, place, and promotion) that also significantly affect what consumers are willing to pay for a product.

CHAPTER OBJECTIVES

This chapter is organized around a series of numbered learning objectives. Each objective statement that follows includes space for you to restate the statement as a question, then answer it with a concise answer that also summarizes the text section.

Step 1   Restate the objective statement as a question.

Step 2   Read the corresponding section in the textbook.

Step 3   Based on what you have read, answer the objective question.

■ CHAPTER OBJECTIVES

1. Explain how different perspectives on price influence the pricing process.

Question

Answer

2. Describe how pricing decisions are made.

Question

Answer

3. Discuss further influences on price.

Question

Answer

4. Describe the four decisions made during pricing.

Question

Answer

5. Discuss popular pricing practices.

Question

Answer

6. Decide if price is an art or a science.

Question

Answer

7. Discuss the interrelationship among price and the other marketing mix variables (product, place, and promotion).

Question

Answer

CHAPTER OUTLINE

I. Explain how different perspectives on price influence the pricing process.

-

-

-

-

-

-

II. Describe how pricing decisions are made.

-

-

-

-

-

-

III. Discuss further influences on price.

-

-

-

-

213

IV. Describe the four decisions made during pricing.

-

-

-

-

-

-

V. Discuss popular pricing practices.

-

-

-

-

214

VI. Decide if price is an art or a science.

    •

    •

    •

    •

    •

VII. Discuss the interrelationship among price and the other marketing mix variables (product, place, and promotion).

    •

    •

KEY TERMS

In the space beside each key term, write your own definition of the term <u>without referring to the textbook</u>.

■ **KEY TERMS FOR YOU TO DEFINE**

Barter

Consumer Confidence

Status Conscious

Price Comparison

Price Range

Price Floor

Price Ceiling

Law of Demand

Necessities

Inelastic Demand

Elastic Demand

Price War

Nonprice Competition

Markup

Cost Plus Pricing

Skimming Pricing

Penetration Pricing

Price Level

Flexible Pricing

Stable Pricing

Price Lining

Break-Even point

Marginal Price

Acceptable Price

217

CHAPTER QUESTIONS AND ACTIVITIES

This section provides you with a place to answer the questions posed in the textbook in the **Check Your Understanding** sections and in the **Discussion Questions, Mini-Cases,** and **What Do You Think?** at the end of the chapter. Space is also provided for your reactions to **Marketing Applications, Consumer Insights, International Marketing,** and **Marketing on the Internet**.

CHECK YOUR UNDERSTANDING

■ **Check Your Understanding 9.1**

1. Describe some of the meanings commonly applied to *price*.

2. Explain this statement: "Price is a matter of perspective."

3. Discuss the various perspectives on price.

■ **Check Your Understanding 9.2**

1. Describe the many factors that influence price.

■ **Check Your Understanding 9.3**

1. Describe the steps in making a price decision.

1. Discuss commonly used pricing practices.

2. Is price art or science?

3. Describe the interrelationships of price and the other marketing mix variables.

MARKETING APPLICATIONS

■ **MARKETING APPLICATION 9.1**

What is the issue raised by this **Marketing Application**?

What conclusions can you draw from this activity about the competitiveness of prices for products? Are there significant differences in the prices between national manufacturer's brands and store brands?

■ MARKETING APPLICATION 9.2

What is the issue raised by this **Marketing Application**?

What conclusions can you draw from this activity about special event pricing? How is the popularity of an event reflected in prices?

■ MARKETING APPLICATION 9.3

What is the issue raised by this **Marketing Application**?

What conclusions can you draw from this activity about age-based preferential pricing? Are they fair? How should price fairness be judged?

■ MARKETING APPLICATION 9.4

What is the issue raised by this **Marketing Application**?

What conclusions can you draw from this activity about loss leaders? Are they an effective way of building store traffic? If several stores offer the same loss leader, what might this indicate about retailer price discounts?

DISCUSSION QUESTIONS

1. Why is it so difficult for marketers to arrive at the *right* price for a product?

2. Following are some of the names used for price. Explain what the consumer gets for each price: rent, tuition, toll, charitable donation.

3. Discuss some of the reasons for the increasing importance of price to marketers and consumers.

4. What is consumer confidence? Why should marketers be concerned when consumers lack confidence?

5. Give an example of the purchase behavior of each of the following consumers: status conscious, price conscious, service conscious.

6. In your own words, explain the relationship between price and quantity sold, as expressed in the law of demand.

7. Milk, gasoline, and urgent medical treatment are examples of inelastic products. What does this mean?

8. Why is the government concerned about the prices charged for products? *Should* the government be concerned about prices? What do you think?

9. What is a price war? Is it good for consumers?

10. Explain this statement: "Price and costs are inextricably linked."

11. What happens if the marketer's price range for a product and the consumer's range of acceptable prices are not similar?

MINI-CASES

■ **Mini-Case 9.1: The Price You See Is The Price You Pay - No Haggling**

In your own words, summarize this case in the space below.

1. Do you think that a no-negotiating pricing policy will appeal to *all* consumers? What types of consumers might not like this price strategy?

2. What is the risk for the car dealer who adopts the no-haggling pricing strategy?

3. Do you think no-negotiating pricing is anticonsumer?

■ **Mini-Case 9.2: To Lease Or Not To Lease: Is There A Question?**

In your own words, summarize this case in the space below.

1. Do you think leasing rather than purchasing a new automobile is a good idea for all consumers?

2. Could automobile leasing be bad for the economy?

3. What are automakers and dealers going to do with all the cars coming back from being leased?

WHAT DO YOU THINK?

In your own words, summarize the issue addressed in this WHAT DO YOU THINK?, then answer the questions.

. What do you think of this oven? Do you think personal use consumers will pay this price? What about restaurants?

INTERNATIONAL MARKETING

■ INTERNATIONAL MARKETING REPORT

What is the issue raised by this **International Marketing Report**?

MARKETING ON THE INTERNET

What is the issue raised by this **Marketing On The Internet**?

TEST YOURSELF

The Chapter 9 opening question is

Why is it so difficult for marketers to arrive at the right price for a product?

What is your answer to this question now that you have completed reading the chapter?

■ TRUE OR FALSE

For each of the following questions, print T (true) or F (false) on the line beside the number.

_____ 1. While personal use consumers often complain about prices, business/organizations rarely make price complaints.

_____ 2. Consumer confidence usually rises when an economy is robust and growing, and falls when an economy slows and falls into a recession.

_____ 3. Consumers often view prices within a range, anchored at the lower end by a price ceiling and at the top by a price floor.

_____ 4. The law of demand finds that when prices rise, demand drops; when prices fall, demand rises; this means that price and demand move in the same direction.

_____ 5. Government pays very close attention to product pricing, often aggressively regulating it, because price is an important factor in the efficient functioning of the marketplace.

_____ 6. The marketer's pricing authority is limited by government through such legal controls as the Sherman Antitrust Act, the Robinson-Patman Act, and regulations set forth by the Federal Trade Commission and other agencies.

_____ 7. Price can be used as a weapon against the competition.

_____ 8. Channel of distribution members cannot add a price increase to a product's base price as they convey the product through the channel to the next member or to the ultimate consumer.

_____ 9. There are many factors that affect price, but seasons are not one of them.

_____10. It is essential to consider what is expected of price before the marketer can set a price for a product or a product line.

■ COMPLETION

Complete each sentence by filling-in-the-blank.

11. _____ indicates the value of the things traded in a marketing exchange, a measure of what must be given up in order to take possession or use of something else.

12. Radio station WKQK (Quack Radio) is exchanging 100 minutes of station advertising time for a combination fax machine, copier, and computer printer from Desk Mate Office Supply Co. This exchange, which involves Quack Radio trading advertising time for Desk Mate's office product is an example of _____.

13. Shelly always shops for bargains, never pays full price, and is very conscious of product costs. Shelly, like many other consumers, is price _____.

14. Qua Chu has three children in diapers. For her, disposable diapers are a necessity; therefore, when disposable diaper prices rose recently, Qua Chu felt she had no choice but to continue purchasing them. In this case, Qua Chu's demand for disposable diapers is considered to be _____.

15. The Super D gas station is involved in aggressive price competition with Crazy Tom's gas station. The two gasoline stations sit on opposite corners of a busy intersection. When one lowers the price by a penny a gallon, the other immediately retaliates by lowering the price at least that much. These gas stations are involved in a price _____.

16. Where price is set to cover costs plus an extra increment to deliver profit it is called _____ _____ pricing.

17. The steps in determining a price are to determine decision _____, _____, _____, and _____.

18. Price _____ means establishing different price points for the different products in a line.

19. Students at Eastern University are used to paying 50 cents for a cola drink in a vending machine and might react very strongly if the price were raised. Therefore, the vendor is reluctant to change the price from what students consider _____.

20. It's August and time for the end of season price reductions n clothing. These price reductions are also known as _____.

■ MULTIPLE CHOICE

Circle the letter of the best answer.

21. It costs $2.00 for an automobile to cross the causeway to get to St. Bel's Island. This price is a
    a. fine
    b. rent
    c. tuition
    d. toll

22. Total cost is
    a. price per unit times units sold.
    b. fixed costs plus variable costs.
    c. total revenue minus total cost.
    d. fixed costs minus total costs.

23. Pete wants all his neighbors to know that he just bought a new luxury car, so he leaves the car in his driveway rather than park it in his garage. For Pete, the high price of the luxury car is a surrogate for prestige and social status. Pete is a ____ ____ consumer.
    a. status conscious
    b. status insensitive
    c. price sensitive
    d. price conscious

24. Pierre is the owner/chef of a seafood restaurant. His prices for fresh fish dinners vary with the cost of fish at market. He knows that when the price for one fish rises, consumer demand for the most part for that fish can be expected to
    a. rise.
    b. stay the same.
    c. rise, then fall.
    d. fall.

25. Cindy believes that only Tide can really get her son's soccer uniform clean. As a result, she always buys Tide even when there is a $1.00 off coupon in the paper for competing brands. Cindy is an example of a ____ ____ consumer.
    a. price conscious
    b. status loyal
    c. brand loyal
    d. product conscious

26. All the drug retailers in Arbuthnot got together and collectively set the prices for a wide range of prescription medicines. This is an illegal pricing practice known as
    a. deceptive pricing.
    b. predatory pricing.
    c. price fixing.
    d. discriminatory pricing.

27. Which of the following statements is FALSE?
    a. Marketers use price to differentiate their products from others.
    b. One of the most aggressive ways of using price as a weapon against the competition is in nonprice competition.
    c. Price can be used as a weapon against the competition.
    d. Different operational areas of a business typically have different perspectives on price.

28. The company's vice presidents are meeting to consider what they want the price of their company's new line of copiers to accomplish. They are debating whether they should cover costs and use a low penetration price or maximize profit with the price of the new line. These businesspeople are engaged in pricing decision
    a. Step 1: Setting objectives.
    b. Step 2: Developing strategy.
    c. Step 3: Determining tactics.
    d. Step 4: Making adjustments.

29. It is the end of the season and Jack has decided that he needs to move out the fall merchandise in order to make room for the winter line. This means he is going to reduce the price of all fall merchandise, using a standard 10 percent markdown. Jack is making pricing decision
    a. Step 1: Setting objectives.
    b. Step 2: Developing strategy.
    c. Step 3: Determining tactics.
    d. Step 4: Making adjustments.

30. Marketa picks up the Wednesday newspaper to look for grocery specials. She sees that the store where she shops is offering two-liter Coca-Colas at $0.79 each, limit 2, with a minimum $10 purchase. Marketa is a savvy shopper and she knows the store is offering Cokes at this low price in order to build store traffic. This is an example of the ____ pricing practice.
    a. predatory.
    b. bundled
    c. loss leader
    d. value added

Note: Answers to the questions posed in this section appear in **PART III: Answers to Study Guide "Test Yourself" Questions** at the end of this *Study Guide*.

CHAPTER 10

PLACE: THE ROLE OF RETAILING

CHAPTER SUMMARY

Retailing is a dynamic activity that continues to change because of intense competition, the volatility of consumer demands, and changes in the environment. The earliest retailers were general merchandisers, offering products of many different unrelated lines in a scrambled merchandise strategy. Specialty stores evolved as alternatives to general stores and offered a limited line but greater depth of products. Contemporary scrambled merchandise stores are often extremely large, with considerable width and depth. Several theories of retail development try to explain why and how retailers change. These include the wheel of retailing and accordion theories. The development of many new retail types illustrates how retailers are trying to satisfy consumer demands for alternative shopping arrangements. These new types include such forms as outlet malls, superstores, warehouse clubs, hypermarkets, and resale shops.

Retailing is an important part of the U.S. economy. It is relatively easy to become a retailer, but many retailers fail. Retailers in the United States generate over $2 trillion in annual sales and provide almost 20 million jobs. Retailing as a whole is expected to grow slowly into the next century. Retailers are categorized by the U.S. government as durable goods stores, nondurable goods stores, and nonstore retailers.

Regardless of retail type, retail tasks are similar to those that were performed in the general store. They include buying, selling and leasing products; communicating information about products, their prices, and where they can be obtained; and negotiating product exchanges with consumers. Because of the intense competition among retailers, they often must change in order to survive. Retailers must make long-range strategic decisions, as well as short-range tactical decisions. One of the most important decisions retailers make is that of location.

Many different retailers typically operate in any geographical area. They range in size and product assortment, as well as along other attributes. One important attribute is that of store atmospherics, the tangible and intangible elements that communicate to consumers what the store is like and the type of products it sells. Store image is how consumers mentally perceive the store. Pricing philosophy signals consumers about the retailer's prices. Service level and form of ownership are other important factors that provide useful information to consumers as well as to competitors.

Some marketers wonder whether or not there is a future for store retailers. While store retailing is very volatile and certainly will change in the next century, it is extremely doubtful that stores will disappear. While store retailing has its ups and downs, nonstore retailing is thriving. Many consumers prefer direct selling because they can make their purchases from home, which saves time, energy, and expense.

CHAPTER OBJECTIVES

This chapter is organized around a series of numbered learning objectives. Each objective statement that follows includes space for you to restate the statement as a question, then answer it with a concise answer that also summarizes the text section.

Step 1   Restate the objective statement as a question.

Step 2   Read the corresponding section in the textbook.

Step 3   Based on what you have read, answer the objective question.

229

1. Describe the evolution of retailing in the United States.

Question

Answer

2. Explain the contribution of retailing to the U.S. economy.

Question

Answer

3. Identify the retailer's tasks and the decisions they make.

Question

Answer

4. Recognize some of the common ways of classifying retailers.

Question

Answer

5. Discuss the future of retailing.

Question

Answer

CHAPTER OUTLINE

I. Describe the evolution of retailing in the United States.

- •

- •

- •

II. Explain the contribution of retailing to the U.S. economy.

•

•

•

•

•

•

III. Identify the retailer's tasks and the decisions they make.

•

•

•

IV. Recognize some of the common ways of classifying retailers.

V. Discuss the future of retailing.

233

-

-

-

KEY TERMS

In the space beside each key term, write your own definition of the term <u>without referring to the textbook</u>.

■ **KEY TERMS FOR YOU TO DEFINE**

Channel of Distribution

Retailing

Retailer

Scrambled Merchandise

Specialty Store

Hypermarkets

Wheel of Retailing

Retail Tasks

Store Atmospherics

Store Image

Product Assortment

Retail Chain

Franchising

Cooperative

Conglomerates

Direct Selling

Direct Response

Infomercials

CHAPTER QUESTIONS AND ACTIVITIES

This section provides you with a place to answer the questions posed in the textbook in the **Check Your Understanding** sections and in the **Discussion Questions, Mini-Cases,** and **What Do You Think?** at the end of the chapter. Space is also provided for your reactions to **Marketing Applications, Consumer Insights, International Marketing,** and **Marketing on the Internet.**

CHECK YOUR UNDERSTANDING

■ **Check Your Understanding 10.1**

1. Describe how retailing has evolved in the United States.

2. Compare and contrast the retail strategies of scrambled merchandising and specialty merchandising.

3. Explain the wheel of retailing theory.

    1. Identify several new retailer types.

    2. What is a resale agent?

    3. Explain the importance of retailing to the U.S. economy.

    1. Describe the types of tasks assumed by retailers.

    2. Discuss the types of decisions made by retailers.

3. Explain the importance of retail location decisions.

■ Check Your Understanding 10.4

1. What are store atmospherics? Why are they important and to whom?

2. Describe the major ways of classifying retailers.

3. What advantages might a retailer achieve by offering products both in a store and through non-store means?

■ Check Your Understanding 10.5

1. Compare and contrast the major forms of store retailers.

2. Why do you think nonstore retailing is growing so fast?

237

3. Is vending machine shopping going to be popular with all consumers? Explain your answer.

MARKETING APPLICATIONS

■ MARKETING APPLICATION 10.1

What is the issue raised by this **Marketing Application**?

What conclusions can you draw from this activity about the assortment of retailers in your city? Can you distinguish between retailers offering goods and services in the same product category? For example, new car dealers and auto repair?

■ MARKETING APPLICATION 10.2

What is the issue raised by this **Marketing Application**?

What conclusions can you draw from this activity about used product retailers in your city? Are there a growing number of used clothing retailers? What other product categories might represent interesting retail opportunities?

■ **MARKETING APPLICATION 10.3**

What is the issue raised by this **Marketing Application**?

What conclusions can you draw from this activity about differences in store atmospherics between retailers in the same product category? Are store atmospherics important? To whom are they important?

■ **MARKETING APPLICATION 10.4**

What is the issue raised by this **Marketing Application**?

What conclusions can you draw from this activity about local trends in retailers offering services? Do consumers want and expect more service, or are they willing to trade service for lower prices?

DISCUSSION QUESTIONS

1. What was retailing like in the early days of this country?

239

2. Describe some of the new retail types.

3. What is the significance of retailing for the U.S. economy?

4. Describe a retailer's tasks.

5. Compare and contrast a general and a specialty retailer.

6. What is a category killer? Explain the name and give examples.

7. What factors are often used to classify retailers?

8. Explain what is meant by the term *product assortment.*

9. Compare and contrast the operations of store and nonstore retailers.

10. What kinds of retailers will be successful in the next century? Why?

MINI-CASES

■ **Mini-Case 10.1: Wal-Mart: Small Retailers' Nightmare?**

In your own words, summarize this case in the space below.

1. Should Wal-Mart be admired as a well-run corporation or criticized for squeezing the life out of small town retailers?

2. What do you think of the "niche around" policy? Will it work?

3. Is there room enough for both a Wal-Mart and small retailers in the same town?

■ **Mini-Case 10.2: Saving Sears: A Retailing Challenge**

In your own words, summarize this case in the space below.

1. How important is image to Sears?

2. What part does store atmospherics play in establishing a store image?

3. J.C. Penney is challenging Sear's up-scale image remake in both the United States and Mexico. If these companies, as well as other department stores like Dillard's, Saks Fifth Avenue, and Bloomingdale's, are also entering the Mexican market, what do you think are the chances that this market will also become overbuilt?

WHAT DO YOU THINK?

*In your own words, summarize the issue addressed in this **WHAT DO YOU THINK?**, then answer the questions.*

. What do you think about slotting fees? Are they harmful? If so, to whom?

CONSUMER INSIGHTS, INTERNATIONAL MARKETING

■ CONSUMER INSIGHT 10.1

What is the issue raised by this **Consumer Insight**?

■ CONSUMER INSIGHT 10.2

What is the issue raised by this **Consumer Insight**?

■ INTERNATIONAL MARKETING REPORT

What is the issue raised by this **International Marketing Report**?

MARKETING ON THE INTERNET

What is the issue raised by this **Marketing On The Internet**?

CHAPTER 10
TEST YOURSELF

The Chapter 10 opening question is

How will retailing change as more consumers gain the ability to shop from home through the electronic marriage of television, computers, and telephones?

What is your answer to this question now that you have completed reading the chapter?

■ TRUE OR FALSE

For each of the following questions, print T (true) or F (false) on the line beside the number.

_____ 1. A channel of distribution is a collection of businesses, often independently owned and operated, that cooperate in placing products where consumers need and want them.

_____ 2. Retailers sell primarily to other businesses and organizations.

_____ 3. Supermarkets have been at the forefront of the move back to the general store concept.

_____ 4. Retailing has changed tremendously in the past but today, because of contemporary pressures and foreign competition, the pace of retail change has slowed to a crawl.

_____ 5. The wheel of retailing is a theory that describes retailers' location decisions as a function of the distance that consumers must travel in order to get to a store, hence the "wheel" part of the name.

_____ 6. Automatic teller machines (ATMs) were the first interactive kiosks.

_____ 7. It is extremely difficult to become a retailer because of the almost unsurmountable financial and legal barriers that a businessperson must overcome to open a retail store.

_____ 8. The Internet is closed to retailers, although many people are trying to get the Congress to change the law that bans retailers on the World Wide Web.

_____ 9. One of the most critical decisions that a store retailer must make is that of location, where to site the retail store.

_____10. Store atmospherics has very little effect on consumer perceptions of a store and its products.

■ COMPLETION

Complete each sentence by filling-in-the-blank.

11. Wal-Mart, Lowe's, Saks Fifth Avenue, Waldenbooks, Lands' End, and a Coca-Cola vending machine are all _____.

12. For record-keeping purposes, the U.S. government divides the retail trade into two segments: _____ and _____ goods.

13. Store _____, the tangible and intangible elements that reflect what a store and its products are all about, include a store's physical design, lighting, noise level, displays, and service.

14. The retail factor that consumers' value most highly is _____.

15. A mass merchandiser offers a very wide but shallow assortment of products in what is known as its product _____.

16. The Thomas family owns and operates 17 McDonald's restaurants in and around Harlan. Although they own and operate the restaurants, they operate under the McDonald's _____, which means that they are allowed to operate as a McDonald's as long as they adhere to McDonald's standards and rules, as well as purchase products from the company.

17. Target, a very savvy retailer, is a consumer favorite because it offers a broad product mix tailored to an area's preferences and low prices. It is a _____ retailer type.

18. Knobb's Shoes, a retail store that sells only shoes, shoe polish, and shoe-related products is a _____ _____ retailer type.

19. Kroger Stores offer a broad assortment of groceries, along with such products as flowers, a pharmacy, perfumes, jewelry, video rental, car supplies, and in some locations, in-store banking. Kroger is an example of a _____ retailer type.

20. When retailers bring their products directly to the consumer's home, it is considered an example of _____ selling.

■ MULTIPLE CHOICE

Circle the letter of the best answer.

21. As retailers become successful, they decide to grow and enhance their image by trading up, improving their store design, charging higher prices, offering more services, and stocking a better quality of products. This is described in the
    a. Accordion Theory.
    b. Give and Take Theory.
    c. Wheel of Retailing Theory.
    d. Theory of Retail Change.

22. Celia loves Sam's Club's low prices, even though she often has to purchase products in bulk, getting larger quantities than she really needs, and must pay an annual membership fee. Sam's Club is an example of a
    a. warehouse club.
    b. supermarket.
    c. discount store.
    d. kiosk.

23. Timmie buys all of his sports equipment at Sports Go Round, which resells gently used equipment at good prices. This retailer is an example of a _____ store.
    a. kiosk
    b. hypermarket
    c. warehouse
    d. resale

24. _____ is a broad category that dominates the U.S. economy, accounting for about 70 percent of the U.S. gross domestic product (GDP) and about 56 percent of personal use consumer purchases.
    a. Durable goods
    b. Nondurable goods
    c. Services
    d. Products

25. Which of the following is NOT an example of a durable goods retailer?
    a. Automotive dealers.
    b. Eating and drinking establishments.
    c. Building materials and garden supplies.
    d. Bookstores.

26. Which of the following is NOT a typical retail task?
    a. Obtain raw materials and supplies for product production.
    b. Obtain a desirable assortment of products.
    c. Inform consumers that the products are available.
    d. Make products available at convenient times.

27. Consumers evaluate store retailers by many different factors. Which of the following is an example of the technology factor?
    a. Store atmosphere.
    b. Clear labeling of prices.
    c. Using modern equipment in the store, such as scanners and computer-based cash registers.
    d. Helpful employees.

28. Which of the following specifies retailer ownership form?
    a. A wide, shallow product assortment.
    b. A franchise.
    c. Non-store based.
    d. Full service.

29. Avon, Amway, Mary Kay Cosmetics, and Tupperware are all examples of
    a. Direct selling.
    b. Store franchising.
    c. Kiosks.
    d. Electronic retailers.

30. _____ _____ is/are an intensive form of product distribution that offers a diverse assortment of products, from colas to foods and flowers, in millions of units across the United States.
    a. Direct selling
    b. Cable retailers
    c. Vending machines
    d. Internet retailers

Note: Answers to the questions posed in this section appear in

PART III: Answers to Study Guide "Test Yourself" Questions at the end of this *Study Guide*.

CHAPTER 11

PLACE: DISTRIBUTION AND WHOLESALING

CHAPTER SUMMARY

The modern channel of distribution is composed of individuals and businesses cooperating to facilitate the movement of products from producers (at the point-of-production) to consumers (at the point-of-sale). Many producers engage in dual distribution, using dual channels to get products to consumers; others use even more channels. Agents are intermediaries with legal authority to act in the name of a manufacturer. Brokers directly bring sellers and buyers together. A wholesaler is an intermediary who sells to other intermediaries, most often to retailers, the last member of the channel of distribution at the point-of-sale to personal use consumers. Distribution of goods and services provides place, time, form, and possession utilities. Distributors perform exchange, physical distribution, and servicing functions.

Channel structure is the form that a channel takes, its length, arrangement, and size. Some channel structures are characteristic of a particular industry. Most channels reflect company attributes, product type, markets, competitors, custom, and conditions in the marketing environment. Channel structure is also influenced by distribution strategy, how broadly or narrowly a product is distributed. The three principal strategic distribution alternatives are intensive, selective, and exclusive distribution. Channels must be managed in order to run efficiently, avoid conflict, and encourage cooperation. While manufacturers were at one time typically the captains of their channels, considerable power has shifted to large retailers. Some channel members exert control over their channels by buying other members through a process called vertical integration. Others buy out competitors at the same level, through horizontal integration. Just-in-time systems are an attempt to make channels more effective and efficient. Reverse channels work to return products to producers for recall, repair, or for recycling.

Sophisticated computer technology, new information management techniques, and the blurring of channel member roles are affecting channels. Like most aspects of marketing, there are many different perspectives on channels of distribution. Consumers sometimes complain about the added costs from distribution, yet are unwilling to accept stockouts and other inconveniences that would occur with a less efficient distribution system. Large retailers view channels as ways for them to achieve cost savings and increase profitability by forcing members to be more efficient. Smaller retailers may believe they are at a cost disadvantage in a channel because of the domination of large retailers who exert their power to their own advantage. Efficient wholesalers view channels as their source of profit. Large manufacturers realize that their days of unchallenged channel power are over, now they must work to cooperate with other channel members and particularly with powerful retailers.

Wholesalers are channel of distribution members that provide retailers with the products they need. They expedite the distribution of manufacturer's products, and provide other businesses and organizations with products. Wholesalers undertake marketing tasks such as purchasing, sorting, accumulating, storing, transporting, and financing products. Wholesaling is an important part of the U.S. economy. Wholesalers are typically classified as merchant wholesalers, brokers and agents, and manufacturer's representatives. There are many subclassifications within the types. Wholesalers make decisions about products, prices, promotions, and markets.

Some people make a distinction between logistics and physical distribution. Others consider them two functions within the same general physical distribution process. Physical distribution moves raw materials and supplies into production and finished products from producer to point-of-sale. Transportation is a large part of physical distribution, but it also includes other activities such as packaging, order processing, inventory control, and servicing. Physical distribution is expensive, so marketers must carefully decide what level of service they need. Company resources, product characteristics, and geography influence physical distribution decisions.

CHAPTER OBJECTIVES

This chapter is organized around a series of numbered learning objectives. Each objective statement that follows includes space for you to restate the statement as a question, then answer it with a concise answer that also summarizes the text section.

Step 1:   Restate the objective statement as a question.

Step 2:   Read the corresponding section in the textbook.

Step 3:   Based on what you have read, answer the objective question.

■ CHAPTER OBJECTIVES

1. **Explain how distribution facilitates the flow of products from producer to consumer.**

    Question

    Answer

2. **Identify the factors that influence the development of a channel structure.**

    Question

    Answer

3. **Describe the different perspectives on channels of distribution.**

    Question

    Answer

4. Explain the role of wholesalers.

Question

Answer

5. Characterize the logistics/physical distribution functions.

Question

Answer

CHAPTER OUTLINE

I. Explain how distribution facilitates the flow of products from producer to consumer.

II. Identify the factors that influence the development of a channel structure.

    •

    •

    •

    •

    •

    •

III. Describe the different perspectives on channels of distribution.

    •

    •

    •

IV. **Explain the role of wholesalers.**

V. **Characterize the logistics/physical distribution functions.**

·

·

·

·

KEY TERMS

In the space beside each key term, write your own definition of the term <u>without referring to the textbook</u>.

■ **KEY TERMS FOR YOU TO DEFINE**

Dual Distribution

Intermediaries

Agents

Brokers

Wholesalers

Channel Structure

Intensive Distribution

Selective Distribution

Exclusive Distribution

Vertical Integration

Horizontal Integration

Just-In-Time Systems

Stockouts

Reverse Channels

Merchant Wholesalers

Manufacturer's Representatives

Physical Distribution

CHAPTER QUESTIONS AND ACTIVITIES

This section provides you with a place to answer the questions posed in the textbook in the **Check Your Understanding** sections and in the **Discussion Questions, Mini-Cases,** and **What Do You Think?** at the end of the chapter. Space is also provided for your reactions to **Marketing Applications, Consumer Insights, International Marketing,** and **Marketing on the Internet.**

CHECK YOUR UNDERSTANDING

■ **Check Your Understanding 11.1**

1. What is a marketing intermediary?

2. Identify the utilities provided by distribution.

3. Describe the marketing functions associated with distribution.

■ **Check Your Understanding 11.2**

    1. Identify some of the factors that influence channel structure.

■ **Check Your Understanding 11.3**

    1. Compare and contrast the three distribution coverage alternatives: intensive, selective, and exclusive distribution.

    2. Are all channels managed smoothly? Explain your answer.

    3. Discuss the use of reverse channels of distribution.

■ **Check Your Understanding 11.4**

    1. What is the role of wholesaling in product distribution?

    2. Describe the different wholesale tasks.

    3. Identify the different types of wholesalers.

■ **Check Your Understanding 11.5**

    1. Describe the types of decisions wholesalers make.

    2. What is the role of physical distribution?

    3. Discuss the different tasks of physical distribution.

MARKETING APPLICATIONS

■ MARKETING APPLICATION 11.1

What is the issue raised by this **Marketing Application**?

What conclusions can you draw from this activity about at least one possible source of friction in a channel of distribution? What steps might be taken to resolve the problem?

■ MARKETING APPLICATION 11.2

What is the issue raised by this **Marketing Application**?

What conclusions can you draw from this activity about education distribution? Is it an efficient delivery system in your area?

■ MARKETING APPLICATION 11.3

What is the issue raised by this **Marketing Application**?

What conclusions can you draw from this activity about differences in channel structure based on the products that are being distributed?

■ MARKETING APPLICATION 11.4

What is the issue raised by this **Marketing Application**?

What conclusions can you draw from this activity about local channels of distribution that supply area retailers?

DISCUSSION QUESTIONS

1. What is the role of distribution in marketing?

2. Why are intermediaries also called *middlemen*?

3. Are retailers members of the channel of distribution?

4. Discuss the utilities provided by distribution.

5. How may the marketing environment affect channel structure?

6. Explain how intensive, selective, and exclusive distribution influence the number of middlemen needed in a channel.

7. What is JIT?

8. How does wholesaling serve retailing? How does it serve producers?

9. Describe the various perspectives on distribution.

10. What are the tasks of wholesaling? What are the tasks of physical distribution?

MINI-CASES

■ **Mini-Case 11.1: A Tasty Case Of Worldwide Distribution**

In your own words, summarize this case in the space below.

1. What advantage is there for CPC in using the distribution channels of brands it acquires in other countries?

2. Why should food products in particular require adaptation to local tastes?

3. Could this strategy of worldwide marketing synergy in distribution be used by other businesses? What types of products might lend themselves to this strategy?

■ Mini-Case 11.2 Ito-Yokado, Lojas Americana SA, And Wal-Mart

In your own words, summarize this case in the space below.

1. Wal-Mart is the first American retailer to open stores in Argentina and Brazil. It is also moving aggressively into Japan and Asia. What are the risks of extending its distribution system beyond North America?

2. How is Wal-Mart countering this risk?

3. Do you think Wal-Mart is on the way to becoming as widely distributed as Coca-Cola, McDonald's, and KFC? Explain your answer.

WHAT DO YOU THINK?

In your own words, summarize the issue addressed in this WHAT DO YOU THINK?, then answer the questions.

. Although the trend appears to be toward consolidations, is there a place for efficient, small wholesalers? What niche can such a wholesaler serve?

CONSUMER INSIGHTS, INTERNATIONAL MARKETING

■ CONSUMER INSIGHT 11.1

What is the issue raised by this **Consumer Insight**?

■ CONSUMER INSIGHT 11.2

What is the issue raised by this **Consumer Insight**?

■ INTERNATIONAL MARKETING REPORT

What is the issue raised by this **International Marketing Report**?

MARKETING ON THE INTERNET

What is the issue raised by this **Marketing On The Internet?**

CHAPTER 11
TEST YOURSELF

The Chapter 11 opening question is

If distribution is so important a marketing function, why is it so invisible to most personal use consumers?

What is your answer to this question now that you have completed reading the chapter?

■ TRUE OR FALSE

For each of the following questions, print T (true) or F (false) on the line beside the number.

_____ 1. The core job of marketing is to expedite the process of getting seller and buyer together so they can make mutually beneficial exchanges.

_____ 2. Although fewer than 20 percent of all product purchases require intermediaries, it is still important to understand what channel members do to facilitate exchange.

_____ 3. Only goods are distributed.

_____ 4. Time utility means making products available when consumers want them.

_____ 5. Physical distribution functions include transporting products as well as storing, holding, and sorting.

_____ 6. The break bulk function requires breaking large bulk lots into smaller assortments that can be sold more efficiently.

_____ 7. A channel's structure is solely the result of the industry to which the channel members belong.

_____ 8. Perishable products like automobiles must be moved quickly through a distribution channel.

_____ 9. An automobile just-in-time delivery system means that because inventory is low, supplies and materials must be delivered just when they are needed for production.

_____10. Channel structures in business and organization markets tend to be more complicated than in personal use consumer markets.

■ COMPLETION

Complete each sentence by filling-in-the-blank.

11. Members of a channel of distribution are also called _____.

12. Retailers usually are supplied with products through the services of the channel of distribution member known as a _____.

13. _____ utility means making products available when consumers need and want them.

14. _____ utility means that channel members provide mechanisms that allow consumers to exchange something of value for a product and take ownership of it.

15. The form a channel takes, its length, arrangement, and size is also called its _____.

16. The simplest, most direct channel structure for personal use consumers involves two members: _____ and _____.

17. A three channel member structure typically includes the two channel members identified in question 16, plus a _____.

18. Making convenience products available just about everywhere possible is an example of a(n) _____ distribution strategy.

19. There is usually only one Lexan luxury automobile dealership in cities with a population under 300,000 people. This restricted coverage is an example of _____ distribution.

20. When a department store chain purchases a trucking company to deliver products to the stores and to customers, it is an example of _____ integration.

■ MULTIPLE CHOICE

Circle the letter of the best answer.

21. Biz Wear is a line of fashionable men's clothing sold in selected department stores in large and mid-size cities across the United States. Biz Wear is using a(n) ____ distribution strategy.
    a. intensive
    b. selective
    c. exclusive
    d. restrictive

22. When Wal-Mart's Sam's Club purchased the PACE Members Warehouse chain from K-Mart, it was an example of
    a. channel narrowing.
    b. channel conglomeration.
    c. horizontal integration.
    d. vertical integration.

23. The movement to return products and packaging back to the producer is very popular in Western Europe, particularly in Germany. This type of distribution is known as ____.
    a. reverse channels
    b. just-in-time channels
    c. product return
    d. packaging return

24. In Japan, Takuhaibin is very popular. It is a form of ____.
    a. just-in-time delivery systems
    b. home delivery
    c. retailing
    d. wholesaling

25. The wholesale task of providing credit and other forms of financial assistance is called ____.
    a. purchasing
    b. accumulating
    c. storing
    d. financing

26. The wholesale task of separating and grouping products into bunches that share such characteristics as size, shape, color, or form is called ____.
    a. purchasing
    b. sorting
    c. accumulating
    d. storing

27. The limited service merchant wholesalers who provide racks to shelve such products as toys and housewares in supermarkets are called ____.
    a. truck jobbers
    b. drop shippers
    c. cash and carry wholesalers
    d. rack jobbers

28. Ensuring that orders are received, processed, checked, and dispatched efficiently is a function of ___ .
    a. packing.
    b. inventory control
    c. order processing
    d. transportation

29. Stokes Industrials has to transport a 50 pound package of special drill bit inserts from its plant in Ohio to a customer in Scotland. Because the company is facing a serious time deadline, it will select ____ transport, despite its higher cost, because it offers a speed advantage.
    a. air
    b. land
    c. water
    d. pipeline

30. In considering the cost of various transportation alternatives, the Ace Coal Co. will avoid ____ transport for its bulk shipments of coal because of its high cost.
    a. air
    b. land
    c. water
    d. pipeline

Note: Answers to the questions posed in this section appear in **PART III: Answers to Study Guide "Test Yourself" Questions** at the end of this *Study Guide*.

CHAPTER 12

UNDERSTANDING PROMOTION

CHAPTER SUMMARY

Promotion is persuasive, purposive marketing communication. Promotion informs consumers, helps build a brand image, persuades consumers to make a purchase, reminds them about products, and even entertains them. Promotion works by breaking through the clutter, grabbing the consumer's attention, and presenting reasons why a consumer should take a particular action. Promotions are used to establish long term relationships with consumers that focus marketing activities on getting close to and connecting with them, and satisfying their needs and wants. Marketing communications are described by the communication process model where a source encodes a message that is transmitted through a communication channel to a receiver, who decodes the message and provides feedback. Noise (interference) from mechanical, technical, and human sources, can undermine if not prevent communication. Marketing promotion is performed by businesses, as well as government, organizations, and individuals. Integrated marketing communication (IMC) is designed from the consumer's perspective and uses many promotion types to deliver integrated, unified, coordinated messages and incentives. It is finely targeted to receptive audiences using information obtained from databases.

Promotion decisions are about which types to use (advertising, sales promotions, personal selling, public relations/publicity, direct marketing), how to use them, when and for how long, using what media. Decisions about promotions are designed to determine how to get the consumer to act, most often to make a purchase. The hierarchy of effects model is used to describe how consumers are moved from awareness to purchase. It is more effective for high involvement product decisions. Consumers control promotions in many different ways, including such activities as selectively perceiving promotions, changing channels when advertisements appear, requesting removal of their names from direct mail lists, using call screening on their telephones to block sales calls, and refusing to buy products whose promotions irritate or offend them.

The promotion plan is a blueprint for action that sets objectives for promotion to achieve and provides a blueprint for doing so. Promotion planning must consider product characteristics including life cycle stage, along with price and place; the competition; target audience characteristics; the channel of distribution; and what is happening in the environment. Steps in the planning process include identifying promotion goals, making promotion assignments, formulating promotion strategy, identifying target audiences, developing the message, selecting the promotion types, allocating the budget, and implementing, evaluating, and making modifications to the promotion plan, as needed.

Promotion budgets are set in many different ways, including such methods as percentage of sales, competitive parity, all that's left, seat of the pants, objective and task, and the use of sophisticated computer models.

Promotion is the element in the marketing mix that blatantly calls attention to itself. It is criticized for being very costly, which adds to product prices, and for its intensity and pervasiveness, which may encourage consumer materialism and conspicuous consumption. Promotion is criticized for being devious and untruthful, misleading, deceptive, overly harsh, and blighting the landscape. Advertising is criticized as being misleading, tasteless, and toxic. Promotion is also blamed for invading consumers' privacy. In defense of promotion, it provides information that can increase competition and lower prices. It subsidizes a free press and provides a public service through public service announcements. Millions of people throughout the world are employed in promotions.

CHAPTER OBJECTIVES

This chapter is organized around a series of numbered learning objectives. Each objective statement that follows includes space for you to restate the statement as a question, then answer it with a concise answer that also summarizes the text section.

Step 1   Restate the objective statement as a question.

Step 2   Read the corresponding section in the textbook.

Step 3   Based on what you have read, answer the objective question.

■ **CHAPTER OBJECTIVES**

    1. Explain how promotion works.

        Question

        Answer

    2. Discuss promotion decisions.

        Question

        Answer

    3. Identify the steps in a promotion plan.

        Question

        Answer

4. **Describe promotion budgeting practices.**

   Question

   Answer

5. **Address criticisms of promotion.**

   Question

   Answer

CHAPTER OUTLINE

I. **Explain how promotion works.**

271

II. Discuss promotion decisions.

III. Identify the steps in a promotion plan.

272

IV. Describe promotion budgeting practices.

V. Address criticisms of promotion.

273

KEY TERMS

In the space beside each key term, write your own definition of the term <u>without referring to the textbook</u>.

■ **KEY TERMS FOR YOU TO DEFINE**

Clutter

Relationship Marketing

Message

Incentive

Promotion Delivery System

Synergy

Integrated Marketing Communication

Promotion Mix

Promotion Plan

Emotional Appeal

Rational Appeal

Budget

Allocations

Conspicuous Consumption

Puffery

CHAPTER QUESTIONS AND ACTIVITIES

This section provides you with a place to answer the questions posed in the textbook in the **Check Your Understanding** sections and in the **Discussion Questions, Mini-Cases,** and **What Do You Think?** at the end of the chapter. Space is also provided for your reactions to **Marketing Applications, Consumer Insights, International Marketing,** and **Marketing on the Internet.**

CHECK YOUR UNDERSTANDING

■ **Check Your Understanding 12.1**

1. Describe the role of promotion in marketing.

2. What is relationship marketing? Why is it important?

3. Explain how integrated marketing communication differs from traditional promotion activities. How are they alike?

■ Check Your Understanding 12.2

1. Can good promotion save a bad product? Can bad promotion kill a good product? Explain.

2. What is the hierarchy of effects model? Does it always accurately describe consumer responses to promotions?

3. Explain some of the ways that consumers control promotions.

■ Check Your Understanding 12.3

1. Why is planning an important part of promotions?

2. Describe the steps in promotion planning.

3. Compare and contrast several promotion budgeting methods.

■ **Check Your Understanding 12.4**

    1. What are some of the criticisms of promotion?

    2. What are some of the positive things associated with promotion?

    3. Describe some of the controls on promotion.

MARKETING APPLICATIONS

■ **MARKETING APPLICATION 12.1**

What is the issue raised by this Marketing Application?

What conclusions can you draw from this activity about promotion clutter? Is it a problem? How do you deal with it?

■ MARKETING APPLICATION 12.2

What is the issue raised by this **Marketing Application**?

What conclusions can you draw from this activity about ways that promotions can be designed to break through the clutter?

■ MARKETING APPLICATION 12.3

What is the issue raised by this **Marketing Application**?

What conclusions can you draw from this activity about consumers' perceptions of promotions? Can they distinguish between the various types? Is this a problem for marketers?

■ MARKETING APPLICATION 12.4

What is the issue raised by this **Marketing Application**?

What conclusions can you draw from this activity about the challenge of designing an integrated marketing communication program for small businesses?

■ **MARKETING APPLICATION 12.5**

What is the issue raised by this **Marketing Application**?

What conclusions can you draw from this activity about the use of celebrities as product endorsers? What characteristics make some celebrity product endorsers more effective than others?

DISCUSSION QUESTIONS

1. If consumer demand exceeded product supply, would there still be a need for promotion? Explain your answer?

2. What is promotion clutter? Identify some sources and explain why it is a problem.

3. Discuss the simple model of the communication process. @T8 = Explain the importance of this model to promotion.

4. Why is relationship marketing of concern to marketers? Can it benefit consumers?

5. Compare and contrast integrated marketing communication (IMC) and traditional promotion.

6. How is consumer insight important to promotions?

7. What are some of the promotion decisions that marketers must make?

8. Identify the types of promotions in the promotion mix.

9. What are the steps in promotion planning?

10. Discuss some of the criticisms and defenses of promotion.

MINI-CASES

■ **Mini-Case 12.1: Promoting Through Sports Sponsorships**

In your own words, summarize this case in the space below.

1. Is sports sponsorship a good idea for every business?

2. The Gay Games IV, which were held in New York City, involved 11,000 athletes, had over a half million out-of-town spectators, and pumped over $100 million into the New York City economy. In the United States, there are estimated to be 13 to 14 million adults who identify themselves as gay or lesbian. As a group, they are well educated with higher disposable incomes than straight consumers; gay consumers are five times more likely to earn over $100,000 a year. The next Gay Games will be held in Amsterdam in 1998. What are the benefits/costs of being a business sponsor for the Gay Games?

3. Was 1994 World Cup sponsorship a good promotion idea?

■ **Mini-Case 12.2 Wilma! A Blowout Of Promotions**

In your own words, summarize this case in the space below.

1. Some members of the film industry are very critical of movies being reedited for marketing promotion purposes. How do you feel about it?

2. Have movie sales promotions and product placements become intrusive or are they effective ways to sell products?

3. Can sales promotions like Barq's and Marlboro's build the brand?

WHAT DO YOU THINK?

In your own words, summarize the issue addressed in this WHAT DO YOU THINK?, then answer the questions.

. Could tobacco sponsorships in the United States be banned? What do you think of the promotion of tobacco products? Are there segments of the population that need greater protection from tobacco promotions? Explain your answer.

CONSUMER INSIGHTS, INTERNATIONAL MARKETING

■ CONSUMER INSIGHT 12.1

What is the issue raised by this **Consumer Insight**?

■ CONSUMER INSIGHT 12.2

What is the issue raised by this **Consumer Insight**?

INTERNATIONAL MARKETING REPORT

What is the issue raised by this **International Marketing Report**?

MARKETING ON THE INTERNET

What is the issue raised by this **Marketing On The Internet**?

CHAPTER 12
TEST YOURSELF

The Chapter 12 opening questions are

How will marketers promote their products in the next century? Will promotion as we know it today via mass media (television, radio, newspapers, magazines) be as prominent?

What are your answers to these questions now that you have completed reading the chapter?

■ TRUE OR FALSE

For each of the following questions, print T (true) or F (false) on the line beside the number.

_____ 1. A common goal of promotion is to make the extraordinary appear to be ordinary.

_____ 2. In the communication model, a source creates or decodes a message, while the receiver encodes it into understandable patterns of thought.

_____ 3. Some promotion is personal, like television advertising.

_____ 4. Marketing promotion is performed by businesses, not-for-profit organizations, governments, causes, and individuals.

_____ 5. Coupons are incentives that encourage consumers to make a purchase because they rebate a portion of the product's price.

_____ 6. The promotion mix is product, price, place, and advertising.

_____ 7. Sales promotions are short term incentives that add value to products.

_____ 8. Advertising circulars are very popular with consumers, grab their attention, and are often taken on store visits.

_____ 9. In the integrated European Union, language differences can easily be accommodated in television commercials by using dubbing and voice-overs on different sound tracks.

_____10. Consumers are completely unable to control promotions.

■ COMPLETION

Complete each sentence by filling-in-the-blank.

11. In the chapter opening story, most of the promotions that Janelle Davis experienced in one day blended into a blur because their excessive numbers created promotion _____.

12. Jes, a customer service representative in the 4 Square Bank, uses his personal selling skills to connect with consumers, learn about their needs and wants, and match them to products his bank offers. Jes is very good at what is called _____ marketing.

13. In the communication process, the _____ creates the message.

14. Juan is intently watching a football game on television when a beer commercial comes on. He is entertained by the commercial, but after a few seconds the cable signal gets scrambled and the remainder of the commercial is lost. This is an example of _____ in a communication channel.

15. The U.S. Army effectively uses sets of words, images, and symbols to persuade college age men and women to enlist. These words, images, and symbols are also called a _____.

16. S&A Promotions integrates and coordinates advertising, sales promotions, direct marketing, publicity, and sales force telemarketing to promote products to consumers. S&A uses _____ _____ _____ based on their knowledge of the consumer and databases.

17. Advertising, sales promotions, personal selling, public relations (publicity), and direct marketing are known collectively as the _____ _____.

18. The first step in the traditional linear hierarchy of effects model is to generate _____.

19. A _____ _____ is a blueprint for action that sets specific objectives for the promotion program to achieve over a designated time period.

20. The first step in promotion planning is to _____ _____ _____.

■ **MULTIPLE CHOICE**

Circle the letter of the best answer.

21. Luis was half asleep in front of the television set, trying to pay attention to the nature program about African elephants. Just as he was about to doze off, the program cut to a commercial and the volume increased suddenly and dramatically. Luis was startled by the increased sound level and became more attentive to the commercial being shown. The advertiser was using increased volume in order to ____.
    a. rationalize the appeal
    b. personalize the message
    c. cut through the clutter
    d. champion the product

22. Contests, rebates, and coupons are forms of ____.
    a. mass advertising
    b. personal selling
    c. public relations
    d. sales promotions

23. Stefaan came home from his business trip to find a pile of mail waiting for him. He started sorting through the various envelopes, mailers, and catalogs selling one line of products or another. These items represent the promotion type known as ____.
    a. direct advertising
    b. personal selling
    c. direct marketing
    d. public relations

24. Sam was shopping for a new computer. The more he shopped, the more he learned about computers. He read computer magazines, talked with sales people, attended meetings of the local computer club, and paid close attention to product advertisements, which he found to be highly informative. Finally, he arrived at the point where he knew which brand best met his needs. Advertising had helped move Sam to the ___ stage in the hierarchy of effects model.
    a. awareness
    b. conviction
    c. liking
    d. knowledge

25. The television commercial was very convincing in showing how even a nearly new no-wax floor needed to be cleaned with Whizzo. Madge looked from the commercial to her floor and decided she really needed Whizzo to restore its shine. When she got to the local hardware store, however, she couldn't find Whizzo on the shelf. She asked the manager and he said he wasn't stocking it, but since she was the fifth customer today who asked for it, he would order Whizzo immediately. This is an example of a ____ strategy.
    a. pull
    b. push
    c. shove
    d. mixed

26. The man and woman stared deeply into one another's eyes as they sat at the restaurant table, sipping hot cups of coffee while a violin softly played romantic music in the background. She sighed and said, "I'm so glad we both love (brand name) coffee." This television commercial is using a(n) ____ appeal.
    a. impersonal
    b. objective
    c. rational
    d. emotional

27. Dart, Inc. is setting its annual promotion budget using a predetermined percentage of sales that historically has been spent on promotions. This is an example of the ____ promotion budgeting method.
    a. competitive parity
    b. percentage of sales
    c. objective and task
    d. statistical model

28. Some critics believe that the intensity of promotion and its pervasiveness encourages consumer materialism, which results in ____ ____.
    a. conspicuous egalitarianism
    b. social consciousness
    c. conspicuous consumption
    d. protective materialism

29. Which of the following is NOT an example of a criticism of promotion?
    a. Public Service Announcements.
    b. Visual blight.
    c. Scams.
    d. Advertising to children.

30. Promotion is regulated in many different ways. Which of the following represents self-regulation?
    a. Federal Trade Commission.
    b. State Attorney General.
    c. American Association of Advertising Agencies.
    d. Consumers' Union.

Note: Answers to the questions posed in this section appear in **PART III: Answers to Study Guide "Test Yourself" Questions** at the end of this *Study Guide*.

CHAPTER 13

THE PROMOTION MIX: ADVERTISING, SALES PROMOTIONS, PERSONAL SELLING, PUBLIC RELATIONS, AND DIRECT MARKETING

CHAPTER SUMMARY

Advertising is nonpersonal persuasive marketing communication, mostly conveyed in the mass media and paid for by an identified sponsor who controls the message. Advertising informs, persuades, reminds, and entertains. It builds brand image, establishes goodwill, and conveys public service announcements. Advertising is often classified by coverage (local, national, international, global), task (commercial, noncommercial, corporate, public service), media type (indirect response, direct response), and consumer target (personal use, business, organization). Many new forms of advertising are challenging the dominance of traditional mass advertising, which has the advantage of relatively low cost in reaching large numbers of consumers. Advertising provides information and image signals that help consumers position competitive products. Annual worldwide advertising spending is almost $500 billion. Advertising has been around since ancient times. The invention of the printing press (mid-1400s) and advances in technology during the Industrial Revolution contributed to its growth. Advertising has become more sophisticated and widely used throughout the world in the latter part of the 20th century. The advertising triad includes the advertiser (pays for it), the advertising agency (makes it), and the media (delivers it). Advertising decisions involve budgeting, developing a creative strategy, developing the media strategy, producing the advertising, implementing and evaluating the results.

A sales promotion adds value through short-term inducements to take action, such as purchase a product, move it through a channel of distribution, build store traffic, and increase sales. Sales promotions may be directed at personal use consumers, business/organization consumers, or both. More is spent on sales promotions than on advertising, almost half of a typical business's promotion budget. Some critics contend that sales promotions undermine brand loyalty by making consumers more price sensitive. Not-for-profit organizations and governments also use sales promotions. Effective sales promotion requires planning, a clear statement of objectives, careful choice of appropriate sales promotion alternatives, and good timing. Cents-off coupons are popular personal use consumer sales promotions, along with contests, free samples, rebates, discounts, and premium incentives.

Unlike other forms of promotion, personal selling establishes a personal link with consumers. Before the development of modern electronics and telecommunications, selling was principally a face-to-face activity, often conducted door-to-door. Today, personal selling is performed face-to-face, on the telephone, and by facsimile machine, computer, and the Internet. The salesperson is a boundary spanner, bridging the gap between company and consumer. Salespeople can establish an immediate and personal contact with consumers, counter objections, overcome sales resistance, and develop long-term relationships that can lead to many cross selling opportunities. A drawback to personal selling is its expense; it is not used to reach a mass market. Over 20 million people are employed in sales in the United States. Advances in telecommunications allow a growing number of industrial salespeople to work at home, linked to their offices by computer, facsimile machine, and cellular telephone. The sales force is an important strategic tool because of the link with consumers and accessibility to important information about the environment that can be transmitted back to the business. There are many different types of salespeople and selling tasks. Sales force management involves recruiting, selecting, hiring, training, motivating, evaluating, and sometimes firing salespeople. Sales force compensation is often a difficult management task because it involves sensitive matters that affect people deeply. Because it is costly to replace salespeople, the business should be motivated to sustain a consistent effort to field a well-trained, supported, motivated, and compensated sales force.

Public relations is the promotion type that establishes a communication link between a business/organization and various publics. Publics are groups of people who have some interest or involvement in what the business does. Public relations works to build and maintain goodwill and a positive image. Sometimes public relations opportunities develop unexpectedly; other times they must be planned and carefully implemented. While many marketers believe that public relations and publicity are interchangeable, others find significant differences between them. One difference is that public relations activities are paid for, often by an identified sponsor, whereas publicity is not. Public relations activities may target employees, stockholders, potential investors, government, distributors, and consumers. It is under intense scrutiny for visible and overly aggressive attempts to put a positive spin on sometimes negative events. Publicity appears in the mass media encoded by an intermediary sender such as an editor, reporter, commentator, or other third party. Therefore, the original event or information about it risks being distorted.

Direct marketing is the promotion mix element that makes extensive use of computer databases and lists to direct mail and telephone offers to consumer targets. It gives immediate response measurement capacity to the mass media through direct print and electronic advertising, can personalize messages and offers, refine targeting, and reduce the waste of contacting nonreceptive audiences. It is measurable, which gives it a distinct advantage over traditional mass advertising. The tools of direct marketing are catalogs, letters, telemarketing, brochures, direct advertising, direct mail, and other forms. It is criticized for contributing to the promotion clutter, but it also suffers because of it. Direct marketing is often criticized for invading consumers' privacy through the compilation and distribution of lists that contain intimate details of consumers' financial situations, personal lives, and purchasing habits. The computer database is the backbone of the direct marketing industry. A list is a prime set of names and addresses identified by specific characteristics in a database, set into order, and compiled in a mail or telephone contact list. The best list is the in-house list, compiled from the names of current or past customers. Other lists can be compiled by the business or are available from commercial list brokers. Direct mail is growing in popularity among consumers. Telemarketing is often called the most irritating form of direct marketing.

CHAPTER OBJECTIVES

This chapter is organized around a series of numbered learning objectives. Each objective statement that follows includes space for you to restate the statement as a question, then answer it with a concise answer that also summarizes the text section.

Step 1   Restate the objective statement as a question.

Step 2   Read the corresponding section in the textbook.

Step 3   Based on what you have read, answer the objective question.

■ **CHAPTER OBJECTIVES**

1. **Describe the role of advertising in product promotion.**

   Question

   Answer

2. Explain how sales promotions are used.

Question

Answer

3. Explain the promotion advantages of personal selling.

Question

Answer

4. Characterize public relations/publicity activities.

Question

Answer

5. Identify the advantages of direct marketing.

Question

Answer

CHAPTER OUTLINE

I. Describe the role of advertising in product promotion.

-
-
-
-
-
-

II. Explain how sales promotions are used.

⬤

　　•

　　•

　　•

　　•

　　•

⬤　•

III. Explain the promotion advantages of personal selling.

　　•

　　•

　　•

⬤　•

291

IV. Characterize public relations/publicity activities.

-

-

-

-

-

-

V. Identify the advantages of direct marketing.

-

-

-

-

292

KEY TERMS

In the space beside each key term, write your own definition of the term <u>without referring to the textbook</u>.

■ KEY TERMS FOR YOU TO DEFINE

Advertising

Advertising Triad

Advertiser

Media

AIDA

Advertising Campaign

Copy Platform

Creative Mix

Media Plan

Reach

Frequency

Waste

Flighting

Continuous

Sales Promotions

Personal Selling

Boundary Spanner

Dyad

Telemarketing

Public Relations

Direct Marketing

List

Churn

CHAPTER QUESTIONS AND ACTIVITIES

CHECK YOUR UNDERSTANDING

■ **Check Your Understanding 13.1**

    1. Compare and contrast indirect mass advertising and direct action advertising.

    2. Describe some advertising types.

3. Discuss some of the advertising decisions that must be made.

■ **Check Your Understanding 13.2**

1. Who are the targets of sales promotions?

2. What are some sales promotion types?

3. Describe what is meant by *sales promotion strategy.*

■ **Check Your Understanding 13.3**

1. Explain the meaning of the term *dyad.*

2. How are new technologies affecting personal selling?

3. Identify some of the activities associated with sales force management.

■ Check Your Understanding 13.4

1. Identify some public relations/publicity tasks.

2. Describe some criticisms of public relations/publicity.

3. Contrast public relations/publicity and advertising.

■ Check Your Understanding 13.5

1. Why is it difficult to define direct marketing?

2. How is a database used in direct marketing?

3. How are direct marketing lists generated?

MARKETING APPLICATIONS

■ MARKETING APPLICATION 13.1

What is the issue raised by this **Marketing Application**?

What conclusions can you draw from this activity about advertisements? Do they show consumer insight?

■ MARKETING APPLICATION 13.2

What is the issue raised by this **Marketing Application**?

What conclusions can you draw from this activity about infomercials? Do consumers like them? Are they fooled into thinking infomercials are entertainment? Are they entertaining? Do infomercials sell products?

■ MARKETING APPLICATION 13.3

What is the issue raised by this **Marketing Application?**

What conclusions can you draw from this activity about the types of products that most use coupons? Do brands in the same product categories compete for price sensitive shoppers by offering coupons? Are the redemption values the same or is there a difference?

■ MARKETING APPLICATION 13.4

What is the issue raised by this **Marketing Application?**

What conclusions can you draw from this activity about the employment popularity of selling? How do people find out about selling jobs? How are they trained? What insights can you draw about personal selling as a possible career choice for you?

■ MARKETING APPLICATION 13.5

What is the issue raised by this **Marketing Application?**

Use the space below to write your news release. Keep it short, concise, and complete. Use your imagination to fill in the details. Imagine it being read over the radio or on television.

** News Release **

DISCUSSION QUESTIONS

1. What are the tasks of promotion?

2. How did railroads, communication inventions, and mail delivery contribute to the need for national mass advertising?

3. What is an infomercial? How does it differ from traditional television commercials?

4. Compare and contrast advertising and sales promotions.

5. What groups may be sales promotion targets?

6. Explain the advantages and disadvantages of using
   a. advertising.

   b. sales promotions.

   c. personal selling.

d. public relations/publicity.

e. direct marketing.

MINI-CASES

■ **Mini-Case 13.1: "Mattress Mack's" Winning Ads**

In your own words, summarize this case in the space below.

1. Can irritating advertisements be effective? Explain your answer?

2. Which media seems to have more irritating advertisements than the others? What is irritating about these advertisements?

3. Would most consumers sit through an irritating commercial?

■ Mini-Case 13.2 Is There A Free Lunch?

In your own words, summarize this case in the space below.

1. Describe some reasons why consumers like free samples.

2. Is sampling a good idea?

3. Do any retailers other than supermarkets give away free samples?

WHAT DO YOU THINK?

In your own words, summarize the issue addressed in this WHAT DO YOU THINK?, then answer the questions.

What do you think of these two promotion approaches? Will they work? Would you participate in either? Why or why not?

CONSUMER INSIGHTS

■ CONSUMER INSIGHT 13.1

What is the issue raised by this **Consumer Insight**?

■ CONSUMER INSIGHT 13.2

What is the issue raised by this **Consumer Insight**?

■ CONSUMER INSIGHT 13.3

What is the issue raised by this **Consumer Insight**?

MARKETING ON THE INTERNET

What is the issue raised by this **Marketing On The Internet**?

CHAPTER 13

TEST YOURSELF

The Chapter 13 opening question is

Do most consumers think marketing and promotion are synonymous?

What is your answer to this question now that you have completed reading the chapter?

■ TRUE OR FALSE

For each of the following questions, print T (true) or F (false) on the line beside the number.

_____ 1. Advertising is the one promotion form that most consumers can identify.

_____ 2. Corporate (also called institutional) advertising is designed to build goodwill for the company or organization.

_____ 3. Historically, advertising is a relatively new promotion type, with the first advertisements dating from about 1899.

_____ 4. Reach refers to the number of repetitions, or the total number of times consumers in a target audience are contacted in a fixed period of time using a particular delivery system.

_____ 5. A flighting advertising schedule continuously offers advertisements at the same exposure level, with no variations.

_____ 6. Sales promotions add value by offering consumers short-term purchase inducements.

_____ 7. Sales promotions are used only by for-profit businesses.

_____ 8. Sales promotions can be used to build goodwill for a business or organization.

_____ 9. Perhaps the greatest advantage of personal selling is the immediacy and personal contact with the buyer, which allows the seller to counter objections, negotiate terms, solve problems, and establish a long-term relationship with a customer.

_____10. Direct marketing is both a cause and a victim of clutter.

■ COMPLETION

Complete each sentence by filling-in-the-blank.

11. The AIDA model, which identifies the tasks set for advertising to accomplish as it moves the consumer to act, includes the steps of A_____, I_____, D_____, and Action.

12. _____ refers to the total number of consumers in a target audience who are contacted once in a fixed period of time using a particular delivery system.

13. A media _____ is a blueprint for which media are to be used, when, how, and for how long.

14. The primary electronic media are _____ and _____.

15. The principal advantage of _____ advertising is the ability to provide rapid consume. feedback, often through a 1-800 telephone number or a mail-in addressed form.

16. Contests, free samples, rebates, refunds, and premium incentives are all considered

    _____ _____.

17. The _____ and the customer make up a selling dyad, the connection by which seller and buyer interact in a personal contact to make a marketing exchange.

18. Such activities as holding press conferences, lobbying, and eventing are parts of the _____ _____ promotion type.

19. The first form of direct marketing was _____ _____, as used by Sears & Roebuck for their popular catalog.

20. _____, using the telephone to make sales calls to consumers' homes is often called the most irritating form of direct marketing.

■ MULTIPLE CHOICE

Circle the letter of the best answer.

21. Which of the following identify the tasks of promotion?
    a. Inform, remind, convince, induce.
    b. Persuade, induce, influence, sway.
    c. Inform, persuade, remind, entertain.
    d. Remind, inform, induce, convince.

22. The non-profit Home for Single Mothers is using advertising in the Richmond city newspaper to raise public awareness about the Home and gain public support for constructing a new educational building, where mothers can continue their high school studies. This is an example of ____ advertising.
    a. noncommercial, local
    b. commercial, local
    c. noncommercial, domestic
    d. commercial, domestic

23. Microsoft used many different forms of promotion to introduce Windows 95, including a 30-minute television program. This entertainment-like program featured a visit with Microsoft's Bill Gates and others associated with the software launch. This type of promotion is called

    ____.
    a. telemarketing
    b. an infomercial
    c. noncommercial advertising
    d. corporate advertising

24. One advantage of mass advertising is
    a. its relatively low cost in reaching a large number of consumers.
    b. it provides direct feedback.
    c. it gives an accurate estimate of effectiveness because of the immediacy of showing the advertisement and the response.
    d. the low cost of using such media as national television.

25. ____ is credited with the invention of the printing press
    a. Benjamin Franklin
    b. Sears & Roebuck
    c. Jay Kordich
    d. Johannes Gutenberg

26. The members of the advertising triad are
    a. advertiser, advertising agency, government.
    b. advertising agency, media, government.
    c. advertiser, advertising agency, media.
    d. advertising agency, government, sponsor.

27. Media contact with consumers who are disinterested is called
    a. reach.
    b. waste.
    c. frequency.
    d. churn.

28. 1-800 numbers and mail-in addressed forms are examples of devices used in _____ advertising to provide rapid consumer feedback.
    a. indirect
    b. direct
    c. corporate
    d. directory

29. Which of the following is an advantage of using sales promotions?
    a. They can generate rapid revenue increases by quickly increasing store traffic.
    b. They always build brand loyalty.
    c. They decrease consumer sensitivity to price incentives.
    d. They decrease promotion clutter.

30. At Jimmy's Ford Car & Truck, the top selling salesperson in November will win an all expense paid, five-day vacation for two to Orlando, Florida. This is an example of a
    a. coupon.
    b. deal.
    c. contest.
    d. rebate.

Note: Answers to the questions posed in this section appear in **PART III: Answers to Study Guide "Test Yourself" Questions** at the end of this *Study Guide*.

CHAPTER 14

EXTENDING MARKETING:
MARKETING SERVICES AND
NOT-FOR-PROFIT MARKETING

CHAPTER SUMMARY

Goods and services are products marketed to personal use and business/organization consumers. Marketing decisions for goods and services include the four Ps of product, price, place, and promotion. A service is an intangible, perishable product of variable quality whose production and consumption are inseparable. Services are offered by businesses, governments, and not-for-profit organizations. Service products often are made more tangible through promotion and other marketing tools in order to provide a visible anchor for consumers to perceive and use in making product evaluations. Perishable services are particularly susceptible to demand fluctuations. As a result, such practices as peak period pricing, hiring temporary employees, and automation attempt to even out demand. Since service production and performance are inseparable, the service provider becomes very important in representing the business to consumers. As a result, careful attention must be paid to the selection, training, and management of service providing employees. Because services are affected by many factors related to their delivery, variability in service quality occurs. Service quality lies in the consumer's evaluation of the performance. Services are classified by factors such as product attributes, consumer targets, provider training, delivery system, and contact closeness. Services have come to dominate the national economy for a variety of reasons, including the increased number of women entering the full-time out-of-home workforce, dual income families with the income to pay and the need for services, the aging of the population, loss of manufacturing jobs, and the stresses and time constraints of contemporary life. Service providers should be trained to deliver good performance in order to establish relationships with consumers. This means that service providers should have the capacity to perform, the willingness to perform, and the opportunity to perform. Service businesses often undertake internal marketing programs directed at employees in order to emphasize the importance of their roles as service providers. In close contact services, the service consumer both contributes to and evaluates the quality of the service provided.

A service is a product whose characteristics must be determined before it can be offered to consumers. Product decisions frequently involve a service and the good with which it is associated. Service pricing requires a careful analysis of what is being priced and its value to consumers. An equipment-based service can be priced like a tangible good. Pricing a people-based service often requires considering service image, service provider reputation or credentials, and the price charged by a market leader and the competition. Place is also important to service products because many services are store based, which means that location and store decisions must be made. Channels of distribution exist for financial and other services. Service promotion often involves personal selling and advertising designed to make the product tangible and establish a positive brand image. Services marketing requires the formulation of strategy and the development of tactics to achieve the goals set for service products by the business. A service advantage is often enjoyed by businesses that use service as the key factor in differentiating their product offers from the competition.

When an organization is designated as a not-for-profit, it indicates that earning a profit is not a primary organizational goal. However, when it comes to marketing, there are great similarities between profit and not-for-profit organizations. For many years not-for-profits wanted little to do with marketing because they believed that marketing didn't fit their organizational image. However, now that competition has increased and funding has grown more scarce, many not-for-profits are using sophisticated marketing activities to raise funds and gain support for their programs. Marketing in the not-for-profit sector involves public and private organizations as diverse as governments, charities, hospitals, politicians, unions, religious groups, zoos, social causes and activist groups.

Many contemporary marketing applications make sophisticated use of marketing tools. For example, health care marketing is growing in importance as for-profit and not-for-profit hospitals and clinics, as well as physicians and other medical professionals, compete for clients and revenues. Health care organizations use marketing techniques to measure customer satisfaction and develop programs designed to satisfy consumers. Many people are their own product. Marketing is used to market professional athletes, artists, entertainers, medical professionals, lawyers, and others. Entertainment marketing is used by symphony orchestras, authors, movies, music companies, and leisure activities. Place marketing attracts tourists and economic development. Some of the events being marketed are sports extravaganzas (Super Bowl, World Cup), holiday celebrations, trade shows, and conventions. Educational institutions market themselves to students, parents, alumni, faculty, and potential donors. The information age has ushered in the marketing of many different kinds of information services.

The marketing concept is an operating philosophy that has customer satisfaction at its core. It requires the integration of all organizational operations in a business to focus on consumer satisfaction. The marketing concept is being applied successfully in the service and not-for-profit sectors. However, there is always room for improvement. When it comes to the societal marketing concept, not-for-profits practice what many for-profits are still debating.

■ CHAPTER OBJECTIVES

This chapter is organized around a series of numbered learning objectives. Each objective statement that follows includes space for you to restate the statement as a question, then answer it with a concise answer that also summarizes the text section.

Step 1   Restate the objective statement as a question.

Step 2   Read the corresponding section in the textbook.

Step 3   Based on what you have read, answer the objective question.

CHAPTER OBJECTIVES

1. Explain the differences and similarities between goods and services.

Question

Answer

2. **Describe the Four Ps in services and the service advantage.**

   Question

   Answer

3. **Recognize the characteristics of not-for-profit marketing.**

   Question

   Answer

4. **Discuss some other for-profit extensions of marketing.**

   Question

   Answer

5. Characterize the marketing concept in services and not-for-profits.

Question

Answer

CHAPTER OUTLINE

I. Explain the differences and similarities between goods and services.

-
-
-
-
-
-

II. Describe the Four Ps in services and the service advantage.

-
  -
  -
  -
  -
  -

III. Recognize the characteristics of not-for-profit marketing.

-
  -
  -
  -
  -

311

IV. Discuss some other for-profit extensions of marketing.

-

-

-

-

-

-

V. Characterize the marketing concept in services and not-for-profits.

-

-

-

KEY TERMS

In the space beside each key term, write your own definition of the term <u>without referring to the textbook</u>.

■ **KEY TERMS FOR YOU TO DEFINE**

Services

Tangibility

Perishability

Demand Fluctuation

Peak Period Pricing

Inseparability

Service Encounter

Variability

Service Quality

Service Provider

Lifetime Value

Capacity To Perform

Willingness To Perform

Opportunity To Perform

Internal Marketing

Not-For-Profit (NFP) Marketing

Fund Raising

CHAPTER QUESTIONS AND ACTIVITIES

CHECK YOUR UNDERSTANDING

■ **Check Your Understanding 14.1**

    1. What is a service? Is a service a product?

    2. Describe the unique characteristics of services.

    3. Discuss why a marketer's and a consumer's perception of service quality may differ.

■ **Check Your Understanding 14.2**

    1. Explain why services have become so important to consumers and the U.S. economy.

2. What is the role of the consumer in the service encounter?

3. Discuss the importance of employee capacity, willingness, and opportunity in the effective delivery of services.

■ **Check Your Understanding 14.3**

1. Explain some of the ways that services are priced.

2. Can services be promoted? Explain your answer.

3. Can a service provide a sustainable competitive advantage for a business?

■ **Check Your Understanding 14.4**

1. Explain how profit and not-for-profit marketing differ.

2. Identify some types of not-for-profit marketing.

3. Are there any not-for-profits that shouldn't market?

■ **Check Your Understanding 14.5**

1. Identify some of the newer applications of marketing.

2. Do all lawyers agree that the marketing of legal services is desirable?

3. Are the marketing concept and societal marketing concept applicable to service businesses and not-for-profit organizations that engage in marketing?

MARKETING APPLICATIONS

■ **MARKETING APPLICATION 14.1**

What is the issue raised by this **Marketing Application**?

What conclusions can you draw from this activity about ways that potentially unpleasant service encounters can be made better for the consumer? Why is it necessary to do so?

■ **MARKETING APPLICATION 14.2**

What is the issue raised by this **Marketing Application**?

What conclusions can you draw from this activity about the role of services in your daily life? Are services important to you? Are you concerned about differing service quality levels?

■ **MARKETING APPLICATION 14.3**

What is the issue raised by this **Marketing Application**?

What conclusions can you draw from this activity about the importance of high quality service to you? In the low quality service example, what do you recommend to improve service quality?

■ MARKETING APPLICATION 14.4

What is the issue raised by this **Marketing Application?**

What conclusions can you draw from this activity about marketing in your city government? Is your city using marketing effectively? If not, what suggestions would you make for improvements?

DISCUSSION QUESTIONS

1. In your own words, discuss the characteristics that make services unique.

2. In the continuum of goods and services, where would an automobile tune-up be placed? A skating lesson? Five-pound bags of flour? Explain your answers.

3. What might a college do to combat demand fluctuations during the summer?

4. Explain how a consumer may affect the outcome of the service encounter.

5. Compare and contrast the evaluation of quality in a good and service.

6. Discuss the reasons behind the economy's shift to services.

7. What dimensions affect a service provider's performance?

8. Why did not-for-profits avoid marketing for many years? Why are so many using marketing now?

9. What are some forms of people marketing? Give both for-profit and not-for-profit examples.

10. Discuss whether or not the marketing concept applies to services.

MINI-CASES

■ **Mini-Case 14.1: Mail Room Outsourcing: A Big Service Business**

In your own words, summarize this case in the space below.

1. What do you think of the rationale behind Burn's service proposition?

2. Do you agree with it?

3. Where else might Burns target its services? Explain your answer.

320

In your own words, summarize this case in the space below.

In the highly competitive health care market, insurers like Prudential of America, Aetna Life & Casualty, and the various Blue Cross/Blue Shields are rivals that seek to sign up consumers, either through self-purchased health insurance or employer-purchased insurance. Do you think that marketing differs between the for-profit and not-for-profit payors?

WHAT DO YOU THINK?

In your own words, summarize the issue addressed in this WHAT DO YOU THINK?, then answer the questions.

. What do you think of prepaid burial plans? Is this an effective approach for the marketer? What are the benefits for consumers?

CONSUMER INSIGHTS, INTERNATIONAL MARKETING

■ CONSUMER INSIGHT 14.1

What is the issue raised by this **Consumer Insight**?

■ CONSUMER INSIGHT 14.2

What is the issue raised by this **Consumer Insight**?

INTERNATIONAL MARKETING REPORT

What is the issue raised by this **International Marketing Report**?

MARKETING ON THE INTERNET

What is the issue raised by this **Marketing On The Internet**?

CHAPTER 14

TEST YOURSELF

The Chapter 14 opening question is

Is there anything that cannot be marketed?

What is your answer to this question now that you have completed reading the chapter?

■ TRUE OR FALSE

For each of the following questions, print T (true) or F (false) on the line beside the number.

_____ 1. Services dominated the American economy even during the colonial period.

_____ 2. All the following provide examples of services: a day care for children, a dry cleaning store, a car wash, and a bank.

_____ 3. Services are rarely associated with tangible goods.

_____ 4. Denise is trying to get to Ft. Lauderdale for spring break but the air fares have gone up so dramatically for that period of time that she isn't sure she can afford the ticket. This is an example of peak period pricing.

_____ 5. When a good is produced, its consumption typically does not occur until a later time, usually without any contact between producer and consumer.

_____ 6. When Luis began his employment as a supermarket checker, he received training in how to operate a scanner and cash register, and how to interact courteously and helpfully with customers. This training illustrates how important customer satisfaction is to his employer.

_____ 7. Good service relationships were the rule in the former Soviet Union. As a result, when McDonald's decided to open a restaurant in Moscow, it took very little effort to find customer contact employees who already knew how to be courteous and helpful to customers.

_____ 8. Service quality is determined by the service provider's evaluation of how good a job was done in serving the customer.

_____ 9. Tax advice is an example of a pure good.

_____10. Businesses are increasingly concerned about the lifetime value of a customer, so greater attention is being given to ensuring that the right people are hired for customer contact positions.

■ COMPLETION

Complete each sentence by filling-in-the-blank.

11. Erik is a customer service representative for the local telephone company. This means that he is a service _____, the person who delivers service to consumers.

12. The _____ sector dominates the economy of the United States, as well as the economies of most industrialized nations.

13. Zvi is terribly frustrated. He wants to do a good job, but doesn't have the equipment, materials, and supplies that will allow him to perform efficiently. Zvi does not have the _____ to perform his job well.

14. Kim's degree in marketing from a top business school indicates that he has the required job knowledge, skills, and education level for his job as a marketing account manager. In other words, Kim has the _____ to perform his job.

15. Sudie has a great attitude about her job. As a branch bank teller, she enjoys helping people and always greets her customers by name and with a smile. Sudie's attitude, personality, and enthusiasm for her job indicate that she has the _____ to perform it well.

16. Achieving a service advantage requires three things: (1) _____ _____, (2) _____ _____, and (3) _____ _____,

17. The local children's burn hospital is organizing a giant "garage sale", with the proceeds going toward the purchase of a new, high technology burn unit. This is an example of marketing being used for _____ _____ purposes.

18. The Commonwealth of Kentucky was highly successful in marketing itself to Toyota Motor Manufacturing, USA. This marketing effort helped attract Toyota to the state, where it built a large automobile assembly plant. This is an example of _____ marketing.

19. Kamdar is responsible for organizing a computer trade show that will be held in the largest convention center in town. He is issuing invitations to computer vendors around the world, informing them of the show and inviting them to register, set up product displays, and staff booths where visitors can learn about a vendor's computers. Kamdar is involved in _____ marketing, which includes the marketing of trade shows, conventions, seminars, and other activities.

20. The _____ _____ is an operating philosophy that has customer satisfaction at its core, seeks to achieve organizational goals, requires that all functional areas cooperate in trying to satisfy customers, and uses consumer research on an ongoing basis to stay informed about changes in the environment and consumer needs and preferences.

■ **MULTIPLE CHOICE**

Circle the letter of the best answer.

21. Which of the following products is NOT a service?
   a. A haircut.
   b. Plumbing repair.
   c. An automobile.
   d. Automobile repair.

22. A good is palpable, it can be touched, seen, and felt. This property is called ____.
   a. perishability
   b. tangibility
   c. inseparability
   d. variability

23. Because a service is fleeting, it often results in periods when demand for the service is greater than its supply. This imbalance is a result of service ____.
   a. perishability
   b. tangibility
   c. inseparability
   d. variability

24. Asif is working at Sears during the Christmas season as a temporary employee in the computer sales department. He was hired to work during this period of time because store traffic always increases during the holiday season, along with demand for more sales personnel. The hiring of temporary salespeople like Asif during Christmas represents a response to ____ ____.
    a. peak period pricing
    b. demand fluctuation
    c. service intangibility
    d. demand consistency

25. Dominique is pleased with the quality of service he receives at Joseph's Car Care Center. Service quality is a function of
    a. zero defects.
    b. product design.
    c. the consumer's evaluation.
    d. tangible attributes.

26. Susie is explaining to Jeannette the differences between a pure good and a pure service. Sudie begins by giving an example of a pure service. Which of the following would Sudie use?
    a. Restaurant dinner.
    b. Hair cut.
    c. Refrigerator.
    d. Marriage counseling.

27. First Republic Savings Bank relies on automatic teller machines (ATM) to provide customer service during the times when the bank is closed. The machine-based service provided by an ATM means that this service could be classified by the nature of its ____ ____.
    a. product attributes
    b. consumer targets
    c. delivery system
    d. provider training

28. Which of the following is NOT a primary reason why services have grown in importance in the latter part of the 20th century?
    a. Increased employment in the manufacturing sector.
    b. Changing demographics and lengthened lifespans.
    c. Time demands of modern life.
    d. Growing numbers of women in the out-of-home workforce.

29. MT Copying Services has begun a program designed to market the business to its employees, in order to develop their understanding of the importance of their roles as service providers. This program is an example of
    a. external marketing.
    b. internal marketing.
    c. lifetime marketing.
    d. societal marketing.

30. There are many for-profit extensions of marketing, some are in settings other than traditional businesses. The marketing of lawyers, dentists, and other professionals is an example of
    a. social marketing.
    b. people marketing.
    c. event marketing
    d. development marketing.

Note: Answers to the questions posed in this section appear in **PART III: Answers to Study Guide "Test Yourself" Questions** at the end of this *Study Guide*.

CHAPTER 15

MANAGING MARKETING

CHAPTER SUMMARY

Marketing managers guide marketing programs and people in the many different activities associated with offering products to markets. Marketers are information conduits, communicating information about products to personal use, business, and organization consumers, and bringing information back to the business about consumers, the competition, and other important factors in the environment. There is no single marketing organization structure that fits all businesses equally well. Recent trends toward flattening corporations, reducing the number of layers of bureaucracy, gives greater power to individuals to take responsibility for their jobs and make decisions. In multibusiness corporations, marketing management begins at the top with a corporate level vice president for marketing. Some marketing managers are responsible for marketing in all of the corporation's businesses. At lower levels, category managers oversee the marketing of entire categories of products with their many different brands. Brand managers are responsible for managing the marketing of one or several related brands. Other forms include marketing managers for geographical territories, consumer targets, or different operations such as personal selling or new product development. Marketing managers are often called mini-general managers because they perform many of the same tasks as a general manager, but only for marketing activities. Marketing activities are also managed in small and mid-size businesses. Marketing management means making decisions about people, money, technology, and materials through the interlinked processes of planning, implementation, and control. The marketing program is all the various operating marketing plans and activities that represent the total marketing effort at a particular time.

The marketing plan is the blueprint for what marketing is to accomplish over a period of time, usually one year and sometimes two. The marketing plan must be compatible with and complement plans for other operational areas. Marketing plans specify product-market matches, marketing mix tactics, evaluation and control mechanisms, and resource allocations. A marketing plan for a small business usually is less formal and complex than a marketing plan for a large company. A large company may have hundreds of different marketing plans operating at one time; a small business may have only one marketing plan. There are many advantages to marketing planning. One is that it forces marketers to systematically address issues that affect business success and possibly, survival. The planning process calls for evaluating the business's customer base. This often reveals that relatively few customers are responsible for most of the sales. This is the 80-20 Rule, where 80 percent of sales are generated by as few as 20 percent of the customers.

Marketing plans are meaningless unless and until they are implemented. Implementation is the activation of a marketing plan, when people, money, technology, and materials are brought together to execute marketing mix tactics and achieve marketing objectives. Implementation requires organizing people to perform marketing activities. Good implementation cannot save a flawed marketing plan. Three key activities involved in implementation are organizing, staffing, and supervising employees. Implementation often is difficult because it involves change and people have a tendency to resist change. Other implementation problems frequently are the result of communication problems and internal disputes over resources.

Control is the evaluation of marketing performance and outcomes in order to learn whether or not marketing goals have been met, and, if not, why not. Controls provide information that can be used to change marketing plans and their implementation. Control is extremely important when the competition is intense because good controls can lead to a competitive advantage by improving the efficiency and effectiveness of marketing activities. Control tracks performance and outcomes using such measures as sales, market share, costs, and customer satisfaction. Many businesses use a marketing audit to determine how effectively marketing is being managed. This audit of the business's marketing activities is usually conducted by impartial external consultants hired for the purpose.

Control results may indicate that things are running smoothly and only slight corrections are needed. In other cases, control results may show that there are serious problems, so a more drastic response may be needed. Some U.S. companies faced with quality control problems have turned to Japanese quality control methods. This includes kaizen, a commitment to continual improvement that seeks to make products and processes better, and thereby enhance quality. Control results may indicate that changes should be made in product and market mixes or in strategies designed to grow the business. Product portfolio models may be used to differentiate the relative market share or profit contribution of different products to the business. While product portfolio models may have descriptive value, their prescriptive value is dubious. Growth decisions in products and markets can be categorized within a product/market opportunity matrix. The four cells of the matrix include a market penetration strategy which calls for increasing sales of existing products among current target markets without changing the products or markets. A market development strategy calls for entering new markets with the same products. A product development strategy calls for changing products, or adding new ones, to existing markets. Diversifying means offering new products to new markets.

CHAPTER OBJECTIVES

This chapter is organized around a series of numbered learning objectives. Each objective statement that follows includes space for you to restate the statement as a question, then answer it with a concise answer that also summarizes the text section.

Step 1   Restate the objective statement as a question.

Step 2   Read the corresponding section in the textbook.

Step 3   Based on what you have read, answer the objective question.

■   **CHAPTER OBJECTIVES**

1. Explain the role of the marketing manager.

Question

Answer

2. Explain the role of the marketing plan.

Question

Answer

3. **Describe implementation activities.**

   Question

   Answer

4. **Explain the function of marketing control.**

   Question

   Answer

5. **Describe how control results may be applied in marketing.**

   Question

   Answer

329

CHAPTER OUTLINE

I. Explain the role of the marketing manager.

    •

    •

    •

    •

    •

    •

II. Explain the role of the marketing plan.

    •

    •

    •

    •

III. Describe implementation activities.

IV. Explain the function of marketing control.

V. Discuss how control results may be applied in marketing.

KEY TERMS

In the space beside each key term, write your own definition of the term <u>without referring to the textbook</u>.

■ **KEY TERMS FOR YOU TO DEFINE**

Marketing Managers

Participative Management

Marketing Management

Marketing Program

80-20 Rule

Implementation

Organizing

Staffing

Supervising

Downsizing

Control

Marketing Audit

Kaizen

Strategic Business Units (SBUs)

Product Portfolio Models

Market Penetration

Contraseasonal Marketing

Market Development

Product Development

Diversifying

CHAPTER QUESTIONS AND ACTIVITIES

This section provides you with a place to answer the questions posed in the textbook in the **Check Your Understanding** sections and in the **Discussion Questions, Mini-Cases,** and **What Do You Think?** at the end of the chapter. Space is also provided for your reactions to **Marketing Applications, Consumer Insights, International Marketing,** and **Marketing on the Internet.**

CHECK YOUR UNDERSTANDING

■ **Check Your Understanding 15.1**

    1. What is the role of the marketing manager?

    2. Why are marketers called mini-general managers?

    3. What tasks are performed by marketing managers?

■ **Check Your Understanding 15.2**

    1. How do marketing plans differ in large and small businesses?

    2. Explain how implementation activates the marketing plan.

    3. What are some implementation problems that marketing managers may experience?

■ **Check Your Understanding 15.3**

    1. Explain the use of marketing control systems.

    2. What is a marketing audit?

    3. How may control system results be used?

MARKETING APPLICATIONS

■ MARKETING APPLICATION 15.1

What is the issue raised by this **Marketing Application**?

What conclusions can you draw from this activity about the employment situation in small businesses? Do you think small business is where you might find a profitable marketing career?

■ MARKETING APPLICATION 15.2

What is the issue raised by this **Marketing Application**?

What conclusions can you draw from this activity about the jobs of marketing managers? What management style would you prefer?

■ MARKETING APPLICATION 15.3

What is the issue raised by this **Marketing Application**?

What conclusions can you draw from this activity about the difficulty of developing effective contraseasonal marketing plans?

DISCUSSION QUESTIONS

1. Why are marketers called *boundary spanners*? Do you think this is an appropriate designation?

2. Contrast the jobs of category manager and brand manager.

3. How are the jobs of general manager and marketing manager alike?

4. Why are small businesses important to the economy and marketing?

5. What is the marketing program? Why does it require careful coordination?

6. Discuss the interrelationship and interdependence of planning, implementation, and control.

7. Explain why ignoring the 80-20 rule can be a serious mistake for the marketing manager.

8. Compare and contrast authoritarian and participative management styles.

9. Could a business exist for long without some controls?

10. What role does marketing play in the consumer's life? In society?

MINI-CASES

■ **Mini-Case 15.1: China Coast Restaurants - Coast To Coast**

In your own words, summarize this case in the space below.

1. Explain how marketing managers may use planning, implementation, and control in determining whether or not to expand the China Coast chain nationwide.

2. General Mills is trying to grow a new business. Where would this fit in the product/market growth opportunity matrix shown in Figure 15.7 (i.e., what strategy is it? Explain your answer.

■ **Mini-Case 15.2 Managing Marketing And The Information Revolution**

In your own words, summarize this case in the space below.

1. How can the information revolution help marketing management?

339

2. How can the information revolution frustrate marketing management?

WHAT DO YOU THINK?

In your own words, summarize the issue addressed in this WHAT DO YOU THINK?, then answer the questions.

. What are some of the ways that small businesses are becoming more efficient? Are there other ways that you can suggest for increasing small business efficiency?

CONSUMER INSIGHTS, INTERNATIONAL MARKETING

■ CONSUMER INSIGHT 15.1

What is the issue raised by this **Consumer Insight**?

■ CONSUMER INSIGHT 15.2

What is the issue raised by this **Consumer Insight**?

INTERNATIONAL MARKETING REPORT

What is the issue raised by this **International Marketing Report?**

MARKETING ON THE INTERNET

What is the issue raised by this **Marketing On The Internet?**

CHAPTER 15
TEST YOURSELF

The Chapter 15 opening questions are

What does it take to manage marketing successfully? Why is it sometimes so difficult to do?

What are your answers to these questions now that you have completed reading the chapter?

■ TRUE OR FALSE

For each of the following questions, print T (true) or F (false) on the line beside the number.

_____ 1. Marketing is the operational area that establishes the most intimate link between a company and its outside environments.

_____ 2. A recent trend has been to increase the number of management levels within a company, adopting the pyramid structure of the vertical corporation, where the company is organized around rigidly defined departments that rarely cooperate or collaborate.

_____ 3. Fortunately, there is one marketing organization structure that fits all businesses, so all marketing organizations look much the same from a managerial perspective.

_____ 4. Marketing managers are regarded as mini-general managers because they undertake the same basic tasks as general managers, although in a smaller, more concentrated, focused operational area.

_____ 5. While there are many small businesses, no single definition is valid for every small business.

_____ 6. Marketing activities must be managed in all business, regardless of their size.

_____ 7. A marketing program includes all the marketing plans that are operating and the total marketing effort at a particular time.

_____ 8. Many businesses engage in marketing planning; very few ever take the time to actually write a marketing plan.

_____ 9. The 80-20 rule states that 80 percent of a businesses customers generate 80 percent of their sales.

_____10. Implementation is the activation of a marketing plan.

■ COMPLETION

Complete each sentence by filling-in-the-blank.

11. David is identifying people who have the capacity to perform the tasks required by his company's marketing department. This includes selecting, hiring, and training them. This process is known as _____.

12. _____ practices are used to determine if a company is achieving its marketing goals. It is the evaluation of marketing performance and outcomes in order to learn whether the goals have been met and if not, why.

13. Moore Products is awaiting the results of a comprehensive examination of their marketing activities that is conducted annually by an unbiased, external firm. This systemmatic examination is known as a marketing _____.

14. _____ is the Japanese principle that is a commitment to continual improvement in products and processes, and the enhancement of quality.

15. Johnson & Johnson Co. at one time had over 100 businesses operating with a high degree of autonomy under the J&J corporate umbrella. These businesses are also known as _____ _____ _____.

16. Star Software's Omega Warp IV Space Game has a high relative market share in a high growth market. According to the company's product portfolio, this product is a _____.

17. Lady Fair Sun Screen is launching a promotion campaign designed to persuade women to use sun screen even in the winter, to protect themselves from the sun's harmful rays when they go jogging or walking. Because sun screen is typically associated with the summer months, promoting it during the winter is an example of _____' marketing.

18. BakeRite Ovens has found a new target market for its quick cook mini-ovens. This is an example of _____ _____ .

19. The Gennen Company is offering a new and improved toothpaste to the same market that has always been the target for their toothpaste. Offering a new product to the same market is an example of _____ _____.

20. In a product portfolio, a product that can be milked of its profits to provide resources for other products is called a _____ _____.

■ MULTIPLE CHOICE

Circle the letter of the best answer.

21. Indar is the marketing manager for Peter's Peanut Butter only. Indar is a
    a. category manager.
    b. brand manager.
    c. product manager.
    d. mini manager.

22. Nice Tires has marketing managers for each major region where the company markets its tires, including the southeastern United States, northeast, and midwest. This is an example of the ___ type of marketing organization.
    a. geographic
    b. brand management
    c. operational
    d. category

23. The Clear Vue lens company has marketing managers for the sales force, sales promotions, advertising, public relations, and distribution. Clear Vue has the ___ type of marketing organization.
    a. geographic
    b. brand management
    c. pperational
    d. category

24. Sid feels very fortunate to be working for the Jackson Flower & Seed Company as a marketing manager. His company views employees as partners who work together in setting goals, making decisions, taking responsibility, and sharing rewards and risks. Jackson Flower and Seed is an example of a company that uses ____ management.
    a. autocratic
    b. categoric
    c. participative
    d. syncrative

25. Which of the following is NOT an activity typically associated with marketing management?
    a. Directing marketing, finance, and production managers.
    b. Formulating marketing strategies.
    c. Planning marketing activities.
    d. Evaluating marketing outcomes.

26. The ____ ____ is the blueprint specifically for what marketing is to accomplish.
    a. category plan
    b. business plan
    c. general plan
    d. marketing plan

27. Which of the following is NOT an advantage of writing a marketing plan.
    a. By addressing each of the key issues, the business confronts issues that can affect its profitability.
    b. A plan can take a considerable time to write.
    c. Plans developed jointly by many people can help build consensus and encourage collaboration and cooperation.
    d. Planning in itself can help a business identify opportunities and threats.

28. The ____ ____ section in a marketing plan is a one to two page abstract of the key points from each section designed to give an overview of the plan.
    a. budget
    b. appendices
    c. executive summary
    d. marketing objectives

29. In the ____ ____ section of a marketing plan, a statement is made of what marketing is to accomplish for the business, including how marketing is integrated with broad corporate and business goals.
    a. marketing objectives
    b. marketing strategies
    c. marketing tactics
    d. control

30. In the ____ ____ section of a marketing plan, a detailed analysis is provided of the factors that will influence the marketing of the product.
    a. executive summary
    b. marketing objectives
    c. marketing strategies
    d. situation analysis

Note: Answers to the questions posed in this section appear in **PART III: Answers to Study Guide "Test Yourself" Questions** at the end of this *Study Guide*.

PART III
ANSWERS TO STUDY GUIDE
"TEST YOURSELF" QUESTIONS

CHAPTER 1

AN INTRODUCTION TO MARKETING

TRUE OR FALSE

1. true
2. true
3. false
4. true
5. true
6. false
7. true
8. false
9. true
10. true

COMPLETION

11. gaps
12. value
13. exchange
14. products
15. marketing mix
16. marketing concept
17. societal marketing concept
18. target
19. place
20. promotion

MULTIPLE CHOICE

21. c
22. d
23. a
24. b
25. b
26. d
27. c
28. b
29. a
30. c

CHAPTER 2

MAKING MARKETING DECISIONS - DEVELOPING MARKETING PLANS

TRUE OR FALSE

1. true
2. false
3. false
4. false
5. true
6. true
7. true
8. true
9. true
10. true

COMPLETION

11. objectives
12. mission statement
13. government
14. SWOT
15. market segmentation
16. marketing plan
17. immediate external
18. international
19. business/organization
20. personal use

MULTIPLE CHOICE

21. c
22. c
23. d
24. b
25. d
26. a
27. a
28. c
29. a
30. c

CHAPTER 3

SEGMENTING THE MARKET: CONSUMER BUYING DECISION

TRUE OR FALSE

1. true
2. false
3. true
4. false
5. false
6. true
7. true
8. true
9. false
10. false

COMPLETION

11. straight; standing
12. gatekeeper
13. derived
14. elastic
15. consumer behavior
16. reference
17. want
18. perception
19. learning
20. attitude

MULTIPLE CHOICE

21. c
22. a
23. a
24. d
25. b
26. d
27. c
28. a
29. b
30. d

• CHAPTER 4

THE MARKETING ENVIRONMENT

TRUE OR FALSE

1. true
2. false
3. false
4. false
5. true
6. true
7. true
8. false
9. true
10. true

COMPLETION

11. society
12. ethical dilemmas
13. materialism
14. ethics
15. laws
16. Sherman
17. Federal Trade Commission (FTC)
18. consumerism
19. John Kennedy
20. green

MULTIPLE CHOICE

21. d
22. b
23. a
24. d
25. a
26. c
27. a
28. c
29. b
30. d

• CHAPTER 5

MULTICULTURAL AND INTERNATIONAL MARKETING

TRUE OR FALSE

1. true
2. false
3. false
4. true
5. true
6. false
7. true
8. true
9. false
10. true

COMPLETION

11. cultural blinders
12. values
13. humanitarianism
14. body
15. ignorance; understanding
16. African-Americans
17. Hispanic-Americans
18. trade deficit
19. North America; Europe; Japan
20. emerging

MULTIPLE CHOICE

21. c
22. a
23. d
24. a
25. b
26. c
27. b
28. a
29. a
30. d

• CHAPTER 6

MARKETING RESEARCH AND INFORMATION TECHNOLOGY

TRUE OR FALSE

1. false
2. true
3. false
4. true
5. true
6. false
7. false
8. false
9. true
10. true

COMPLETION

11. overload
12. information system
13. primary
14. internal company
15. identify; problem
16. exploratory
17. validity
18. focus
19. scanner
20. virtual

MULTIPLE CHOICE

21. b
22. a
23. d
24. d
25. a
26. b
27. c
28. d
29. c
30. b

• CHAPTER 7

UNDERSTANDING PRODUCT

TRUE OR FALSE

1. false
2. true
3. false
4. true
5. false
6. true
7. true
8. true
9. true
10. false

COMPLETION

11. overpackaging
12. patents; trademarks or trademarks; patents
13. cannibalized
14. extension
15. store
16. brand
17. image
18. strategy
19. potential
20. convenience

MULTIPLE CHOICE

21. a
22. c
23. a
24. d
25. c
26. b
27. b
28. c
29. a
30. a

• CHAPTER 8

PRODUCT PROCESSES

TRUE OR FALSE

1. false
2. true
3. true
4. true
5. false
6. true
7. false
8. false
9. true
10. false

COMPLETION

11. acquire
12. test
13. commercialization
14. awareness
15. fad
16. preintroduction
17. perceptual
18. reposition
19. category
20. recall

MULTIPLE CHOICE

21. d
22. a
23. a
24. c
25. c
26. b
27. d
28. a
29. b
30. d

• CHAPTER 9

UNDERSTANDING PRICE

TRUE OR FALSE

1. false
2. true
3. false
4. false
5. true
6. true
7. true
8. false
9. false
10. true

COMPLETION

11. price
12. barter
13. sensitive
14. inelastic
15. war
16. cost plus
17. objectives, strategy, tactics, adjustments
18. lining
19. customary
20. markdowns

MULTIPLE CHOICE

21. d
22. b
23. a
24. d
25. c
26. c
27. b
28. a
29. d
30. c

• CHAPTER 10
PLACE: THE ROLE OF RETAILING

TRUE OR FALSE

1. true
2. false
3. true
4. false
5. false
6. true
7. false
8. false
9. true
10. false

COMPLETION

11. retailers
12. durable; non-durable
13. atmospherics
14. time
15. mix
16. franchise
17. discount
18. limited line
19. supermarket
20. direct

MULTIPLE CHOICE

21. c
22. a
23. d
24. c
25. b
26. a
27. c
28. b
29. a
30. c

• CHAPTER 11
PLACE: DISTRIBUTION AND WHOLESALING

TRUE OR FALSE

1. true
2. false
3. false
4. true
5. true
6. true
7. false
8. false
9. true
10. false

COMPLETION

11. intermediaries
12. wholesale
13. time
14. possession
15. structure
16. producer; consumer
17. wholesaler
18. intensive
19. exclusive
20. vertical

MULTIPLE CHOICE

21. b
22. c
23. a
24. b
25. d
26. b
27. d
28. c
29. a
30. a

• CHAPTER 12
UNDERSTANDING PROMOTION

TRUE OR FALSE

1. false
2. false
3. false
4. true
5. true
6. false
7. true
8. true
9. true
10. false

COMPLETION

11. clutter
12. relationship
13. source
14. noise
15. messages
16. integrated marketing communication
17. promotion mix
18. awareness
19. promotion plan
20. identify promotion goals

MULTIPLE CHOICE

21. c
22. d
23. c
24. b
25. a
26. d
27. b
28. c
29. a
30. c

• CHAPTER 13

THE PROMOTION MIX: ADVERTISING, SALES PROMOTIONS, PERSONAL SELLING, PUBLIC RELATIONS, AND DIRECT MARKETING

TRUE OR FALSE

1. true
2. true
3. false
4. false
5. false
6. true
7. false
8. true
9. true
10. true

COMPLETION

11. awareness; interest; desire
12. reach
13. plan
14. television; radio
15. direct
16. sales promotions
17. salesperson
18. public relations
19. direct mail
20. telemarketing

MULTIPLE CHOICE

21. c
22. a
23. b
24. a
25. d
26. c
27. b
28. b
29. a
30. c

• CHAPTER 14

EXTENDING MARKETING: MARKETING SERVICES AND NOT-FOR-PROFIT MARKETING

TRUE OR FALSE

1. false
2. true
3. false
4. true
5. true
6. true
7. false
8. false
9. false
10. true

COMPLETION

11. provider
12. service
13. opportunity
14. capacity
15. willingness
16. consumer insight; trained employee; constant monitoring
17. fund raising
18. place
19. event
20. marketing concept

MULTIPLE CHOICE

21. c
22. b
23. a
24. b
25. c
26. d
27. c
28. a
29. b
30. b

• CHAPTER 15

MANAGING MARKETING

TRUE OR FALSE

1. true
2. false
3. false
4. true
5. true
6. true
7. true
8. false
9. false
10. true

COMPLETION

11. staffing
12. control
13. audit
14. Kaizen
15. strategic business units
16. star
17. contraseasonal
18. market penetration
19. product development
20. cash cow

MULTIPLE CHOICE

21. b
22. a
23. c
24. c
25. a
26. d
27. b
28. c
29. a
30. d